Angling in France

With

Phil Pembroke

Angling in France
Author – Phil Pembroke
Copyright Philip Pembroke 2004
Published by Phil Pembroke 2004
ISBN 0-9546924-2-X

ANGLING IN FRANCE

France is organised into 92 separate *départements*. **Pêche Francaise** covers the major rivers and lakes, with easy public access in 14 individual angling regions spread evenly over the whole of France.

For each fishing area you choose to visit I provide useful information on night fishing, disabled access zones and details on where to purchase your French angling license, bait and tackle. In addition I explain what there is to do when you are not fishing, and what your friends and family can do when you are. E.g. *Écoles de pêche* fishing schools.

Écoles des Pêche are a feature of French angling life. They are mentioned in this Guide for each region and are not just intended for youngsters wanting to learn to fish but cater for anglers of all ages and ability. Have you ever wanted to learn fly-fishing? Well you can whilst on an angling holiday in France.

There is something for everyone. Many waters are just a short drive from your popular holiday resorts and are suitable for the whole family. For the pleasure angler entertaining fishing sport is available in the most popular tourist destinations of France e.g. Dordogne, Vendee, Cote d'Azur, Loire valley and Paris.

For the dedicated angler the Rivers Somme and Marne less than 3 hours drive from Calais offer all round coarse fishing pleasure. For those wanting to combine culture with fishing, the great Chateaus of the Loire valley form an uplifting backdrop to superb coarse angling on the Rivers Loire and Cher.

Further afield, remember France is a big country, catch enormous *silure* catfish at hotspots mentioned along the River Saône at Burgundy and Lyon. Or why not join many top European carp anglers for superb fishing sport in the undiscovered region of Aveyron in the south near Toulouse. You won't return disappointed!

Dedicated French anglers, experts in their own right offer the reader unique advice and guidance on the best places to fish in their particular regions.

CONTENTS

WELCOME TO FRANCE

France is five times the size of England. On the menu are 235'000km of rivers, 15'000km of streams, 50'000ha of lakes, 30'000ha of *retenues de barrages*, 30'000ha of canals and reservoirs. It is considered by many to offer some of the best angling sport in Europe. 2 million French anglers can vouch for that.

75 species of fish in all are represented. Some will be a new experience e.g. big *silure* catfish, *amour blanc* carp, five different species of sturgeon, *perche soleil* and American wide mouth Black bass. Large zander are caught in great numbers everywhere. In France the size of carp reach the same value in kilos as pounds in the U.K.!

Families may take pleasure from the simple delights of spinning on lovely summers evenings for easy to catch perch by the banks of the calm River Lot near Cahors. A French angling experience takes many forms.

Unbeknown to many there lurk nearby giant *silure* catfish, which are only too willing to make an easy meal of any budding 5 years old angler. And in the *Étang de Suresnes* (*Bois de Boulogne* - Paris) there lurks a Caiman crocodile. So watch out! At *Lac de Tanchet* on the *Vendee* tourist coast keep an eye out for the surfers just a few metres from some super carp fishing.

The scale of some waters is much larger than those used to fishing in the U.K. A boat is an advantage, electric trolling motors and sonar come into their own on *Lac de Salagou* near Montpellier. My tip is to purchase a sack of cattle feed from the local farm co-op and mix in your flavour concentrates and fish offal to create a cheap but effective ground bait mix.

French carp or American cyclist Lance Armstrong, what would you choose? 5 laps around the Champs Élysées after a grueling, 3-week national bike, stage-race or: relaxing by the calm banks of Paris' River Seine in expectation of some great fishing? Then think of the results: personal best fish, *Triumphal* backdrop, get the picture.

A-Z OF ANGLING IN FRANCE

- Ablette –bleak
- Alose - shad
- Amour blanc- carp species
- l'Anglaise – English style
- Anguille – eel
- Appat – live bait
- Apron – spinned loach
- Asticots - maggots
- Barbeau Méridional– barbel
- Barrage – dam wall/sluice gate, weir
- Bar - bass
- Bouillettes - boilies
- Bief – river stretch
- Brème – bream
- Brochet – pike
- Carnassier- pike, perch and zander
- Carasin – crucian carp
- Carpe commune – common carp
- Carpe mirror / cuir – mirror / leather carp
- Chevesne – chub
- Comme appât/amorce - bait
- Corégone – Swiss char
- Cuirs – leather carp
- Cuillers ondulantes – spoon (wobbler)
- Cuiller tournante – spinner
- Digue – dam wall/water barrier
- Écluse – lock
- Embouchure – inlet
- Épinoche – stickleback
- Esturion - sturgeon
- Étang – lake
- Fève – broad bean
- Friture – pole fishing for small fry
- Gardon – roach
- Gougon- gudgeon
- Hameçon – fish hook
- Hotu – large dace type
- Lancer - spinning
- Loup – black bass
- Mais - sweetcorn
- Montures a poisson mort – dead baiting
- Mouche - fly
- Mulet blanc – white mullet
- Noeuds - hooks
- Omble chevalier – char
- Ombre – grayling
- Ouvrages – water works
- Pêcheur - fisherman
- Pépinères – fish nursery
- Perche – perch
- Perche soleil – sun fish
- Petit vifs – small fry livebait
- Plans d'eau –water park
- Poisson blanc – roach/skimmers etc
- Poisson-chat –American
- Pomme de terre - potato
- Retenue – water behind dam
- Rotengle – rudd
- Ruisseau – stream
- Sandre – zander
- Vairon - minnow
- Vandoise - dace
- Vanne – sluice gate
- Vers – worm
- Silure Glane– Wels catfish

LICENSES AND REGULATIONS

The **Carte de Pêche** is the French national angling license However France is famous for its bureaucratic tradition (*un imbroglio juridique*) and when it comes to angling regulations they don't disappoint. The number of different types available almost makes one feel sorry for the *pêcheur Francais*. Luckily the visitor is spared its worst excesses.

This is what you do. Most anglers from the U.K. will purchase the **Carte de Pêche vacances.** This allows fishing for a 15 consecutive day period in lakes and rivers of both 1st and 2nd catagories, usually from June to September. It can be obtained from tackle shops, local bars, Décathlon national sports chain (English spoken) and regional angling associations. Remember to take along a passport photo and I.D. If no French is spoken present a photo of your self, holding a fish and they will get the idea.

The **Carte Journaliere** is a day ticket it is usually available only for the summer months but often available all year. Under 16's qualify for the **Carte Jeune,** which is usually half price. Under 12's often go for free but are still obligated to obtain a *Carte de Pêche*.

Outside the summer months a yearly French angling license is required. What you must ask for is *une Carte de Pêche pour la carpe uniquement, sil vous plait.* By asking in this way you make it clear that that you are fishing purely for carp. Otherwise you will be charged more for the use of unnecessary 1st catagorie trout waters. If you also wish to fish for pike and zander then ask for that additional stamp.

A standard *Carte de Pêche* and the stamp that indicates that you have paid the French fishing tax for one *département* area will cost you approx. 55 euros and entitles you to fish all of the public lakes and rivers within that *département*. You can also buy reciprocal stamps that allow you to fish the public waters in all the bordering *départements* . These cost just a little more. It is recommended that you buy this additional stamp as it opens up the fishing in more than half the *départements* in France. It is called the *Entent Haliautique et Grand Ouest*. This entitles you to fish no less than 55 other *départements* throughout southern, central and northwest France.

The annual *Carte de pêche* is divided into public areas for everyone and private, local angling club waters. And again, into 1st catagorie waters for trout and salmon fishing. But not exclusively. Fishing for zander, pike, perch and carp are permitted on many of these waters but only having paid for the 1st catagorie stamp in your *Carte de Pêche*. The trout season runs from 13th March to 19th September.

2nd catagorie waters are for coarse fishing. The coarse season is all year. The exceptions are pike and zander (*carnisseurs*) fishing in 1st and 2nd catagorie waters where a close season operates in spring and is stated for each section.

Fishing, and night fishing areas (*parcours de pêche de nuit*) are denoted in France by *Lots*, these are simply a way of dividing up rivers into manageable sections and its order is sequential e.g. lot 18, lot 19 and so on. Night fishing sections are sub-divided into smaller *PK, kilometre* markers, e.g. PK 8,500. Don't get too carried away with *kilometre* markers and lots; on the ground, night fishing zones are clearly signposted by the bankside.

PARIS

Angling information: Fédération de Paris de Pêche
4&6 Rue Etiennee Polet
94270 Le Kremlin Bicete
tel, 0153141980, fax, 0153141981
email: fppma75@club-internet.fr

115km of 2nd catagorie rivers, 180ha of lakes and reservoirs, 9,549 registered anglers.

Over the last decade the River Seine in Paris has become a class act. Pollution has been all but eradicated thanks to the efforts of Jaques Chirac (former mayor of Paris) and the *L'Agence de l'Eau Seine-Normandie,*. This improvement together with the introduction of aquatic fauna has restored to the French capital a level of angling sport not seen since the reign of Charlemagne.

There are now 32 fish species present. 18 are caught on a regular basis.

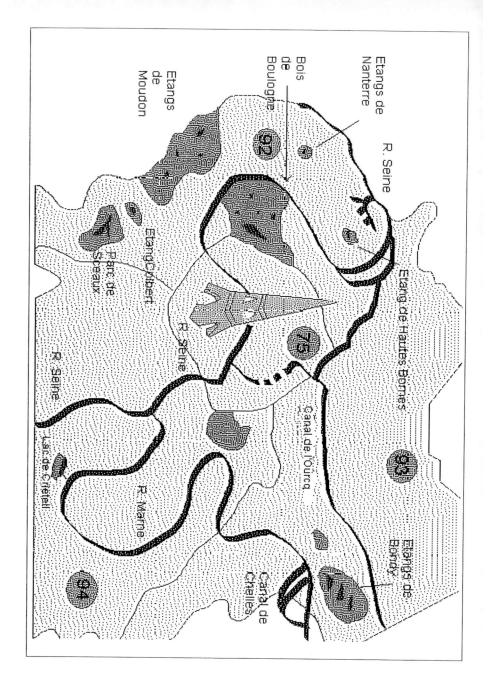

Etangs de
Nanterre

R. Seine

Bois
de
Boulogne

Etang de Hautes Bornes

Etangs
de
Moudon

EtangColbert

Parc de
Sceaux

R. Seine

R. Seine

Canal de l'Ourcq

Etangs de
Bondy

Lac de Créteil

R. Marne

Canal de
Chelles

Where can you fish?

In *Département* nos 75, 92, 93 and 94 there are 250km of waterways to fish. Including the River Seine, River Marne, Le Canal de Challes, Le Canal de l'Ourcq, Le Canal St Martin (carp to 15kg), Le Canal St Denis, l'Yerres and Le Réveillon. For more information, contact the FPPMA, tel, 01 53 141980. **More technically**:

  a) On all 1st categorie public waters (trout): around Paris at, Haute-de Seine, Seine-Saint-Denis, Val-de-Marne. 5% of total waters.
  b) On all 2nd categorie public waters (general coarse angling): around Paris at, Haute-de Seine, Seine-Saint-Denis, Val-de-Marne. 95% of total waters. Fishing permitted all year except: pike close season, which runs from last Sunday in January to 3rd Saturday in April. Rainbow trout season runs from 4th Saturday in March to 1st Sunday in October.

In the river Seine there are mostly common carp to 8kg, this represents very good fishing sport, bigger mirror carp patrol in smaller groups. The pillars of many bridges are well known hot spots. Catch big carp from *Les Quars* in central Paris. A fish of 15kg is not that uncommon, a 20kg carp was recently caught with the Eiffel Tower as a backdrop. Other hot spots include the *barrage de Suresnes*, *barrage d'Alfortville* and *Pont d'Ivry*.

You can now catch pike and zander on the river Seine's city embankments by the *Ille de la Jatte*. Underneath the *Pont de Levallois* carp to 20 kilos, *poisson blanc* and tench to all sizes patrol just below the surface. *Gardons* and *ablettes*, large and small, school by the *Maison de la Pêche* under the noses of big *silure* catfish.

In addition, fish the Seine de Port de Paris at Bougival; there is 70km of bank side to fish in the *Département* of Haute de-Seine.

For additional information go to:	Agence de l'Eau Seine-Normandie
	51, rue Salvador Allende
	92027 Nanterre Cedex
	Tél. : 01 41 20 16 00
	Fax : 01 41 20 16 09

Licenses and Regulations

Make sure you have a license because all the waters are safely baliffed. Ask either for the *Carte Vacance* during the summer, or *Carte Journaliere* (day ticket). If you visit at other times you may require a full priced *Carte de Pêche*, angling license. Under 16's are always discounted.

The **Carte de Pêche Vacances** for the Seine area costs 30 Euros, it covers fishing for 15 consecutive days during the summer, with 4 rods on the rivers Seine, Marne and Caneaux. And includes the right to night fish in designated zones. Types of fishing include coarse, spinning and fly-fishing, on 1st and 2nd category waters.

Carte de Pêche Vacances etangs costs 30 euros, allows fishing with 3 rods on all the Apnle lakes for a 15 day period during the summer.

Carte de Pêche Journaliere is valid for one day only. Carte journaliere River Seine costs 10 Euros, it gives you the right to fish coarse, fly, spinning, night fishing and fly with 4 rods on the rivers Seine, Marne and Canaux.

Carte de PêcheJournaliere Etangs costs 10 Euros, valid for one day allows fishing with 3 rods, all styles except fly, on the lakes controled by Apnle.

Carte Journaliere Mouche Upif costs 13 euros is valid for one day and permits fly-fishing on the trout lakes belonging to Upif; with 3 fish limit. Can be obtained through Club Mouchee APNLE.

It is permitted to fish from ½ hour before sunrise to ½ hour after sunset. Except for carp and eel; which can be caught at night when in pocession of the tax supplement to your *Carte de Pêche* (*carte de pêche de l'Association gestionnare* compulsory.). Outside of the summer months.

You can fish up to 4 rods on all, of the public angling areas in Paris and *crown domaine petit couranne* (inner suburbs of Paris). All rivers and channels are classified 2nd catagorie public, for more information - tel, 0153 141980, or email: FPPMA75@club_internet.fr (for fishing in Départements nos 75,93,94).

Where do I obtain my *Carte Pêche*? **Paris**: *Go Sport Rivoli, 10, Rue Boucher 75001 Paris* - tel, 01.55.34.34.03. **Hautes de Seine**: *Décathlon Nanterre, Place de la Boule - Rue Joliot Curie 92000 Nanterre* - tel, 0141379797. Licenses are available at most *articles de pêche* tackle shops, *tabac-presse* newsagents, all Décathlon sports stores, and local branches of Aappma angling federations.

Night fishing is permitted on the following river zones.

Domaines public – Val-de-Marne area

Sections of the River Seine: restricted to the main arm of the River Seine from the *Barrage de Suresnes* to the *Pont d'Asnières* in total. In particular:

a) From the *Rue de Port* under the *Pont de Villeneuve-Saint-Georges* to the *Pont de la Ligne SNCF* opposite *la Rue de la Marne*, right bank. (*Appma La Brochet de Villaneuve*).
b) From Villaneuve-le-Roi/Orly to the *barrage du Port a l'Anglais* (right bank). And from Villaneuve-Saint-Georges to the *barrage du Port a l'Anglais* (right bank, *Appma La Gaule de Choisy*),
c) The *barrage du Port a l'Anglais* to the *Pont du Péripherique* downstream on both banks. (I.C.A.V.)

Sections of the River Marne.

a) At Maisons-Alfort, river Marne, right bank from the 3rd motorway junction to right of the point downstream, of the *l'Île du Moulin Brûle*, also *Île de Charenton-neau (I.C.A.V.)*.
b) Railway bridge of *Grande Leinture* (facing the road of *Plage a Champigny*. To the *Pont de Champigny* spanning both rivers (river Varenne and river Champigny).
c) 420 metres upstream of *Pont RER/Saint Maur* to 50 metres upstream of the inlet, at *l'écluse Gréteil*, on both banks. And 450 metres of the joint base of the southern and central wet docks of the *port du Bonneuil,* on left bank.
d) Limit of the *départment* of Val-de-Marne with that of La Seine-Saint-Denis (*Rue de Canal*), to the *Grande Ceinture de Saint-Maur* railway-bridge, on both banks.

Étangs of the *APNLE* (Bois de Boulogne and Hauts-de-Seine, 1st and 2nd catagorie public waters).

Lake regulations

Fisheries are open throughout the year, ½ hour before dawn and ½ hour after dusk. Fishing with 3 lines allowed. No nightfishing. Stick within designated angling zones. Lakes are closed in December for re-stocking. Bois de Boulogne (dept. 75). Choosing the right swim is important on all of these shallow lakes, the carp are sensitive to changes in water temperature.

Lac Superieur, 3 ha –A good family water with lots of promenaders on right bank. Left bank is less accessible as there is no path, however this side offers undisturbed fishing and access here for the first time angler is ok.1 –2m deep, this is a good venue for *poisson blanc*, and the occassional pike and zander. Model boats relegate anglers to a restricted area on weekends and public holidays, so it maybe better to visit during the week. **Directions**: by car – via *Porte de Passy: carrefour des Cascades* via *Porte d'Autiel. Avenue d'Hippodrome. Metro – ligne 10: Porte d'Autiel, ligne 9: La Muette. Bus – PC! - 32-63.*

Lac Interieur, 11 ha- closes at 2pm from 1st June to 30th September. The biggest lake in the park, it has carp reaching 20-25kg. More usually less than 15kg. Silver grass carp are stocked, to feed on green algae, some reach 15kg. 3 rod limit. 1.4-2.5m deep, ca, si, pi, pe, ee, p/b, no night fishing at present. Fish for pike and zander at *arbe a sandres* and for carp hotspot visit tail end of lake. **Directions**: by car - go via *Porte Dauhpine* by way of *route de Suresnes* for *Porte de la Muette*. Via *Porte de Passy: carreour des Cascades*. Good car park and easy access to lake. *Metro – ligne 9:* for *Porte Dauphine, ligne 9: La Muette*. By bus – PC1 –32 –63.

Lac Saint James, 2.3 ha – **disabled access**, *friture* is best but also carp, pike and zander. Promenaders on weekends and Wednesdays. For the kiddies there is *École de pêche* and *centre de loisirs*. Pi, za, ca, pe, tr, p/b, 1.8-3m deep. **Directions**: near *Jardin d'Acclimatation. Bd du Commandent. Charcot Route de la Porte St James. Avenue du Mahatma Ghandi. Metro – Ligne 1: Sablons. Bus – 43 – 93.*

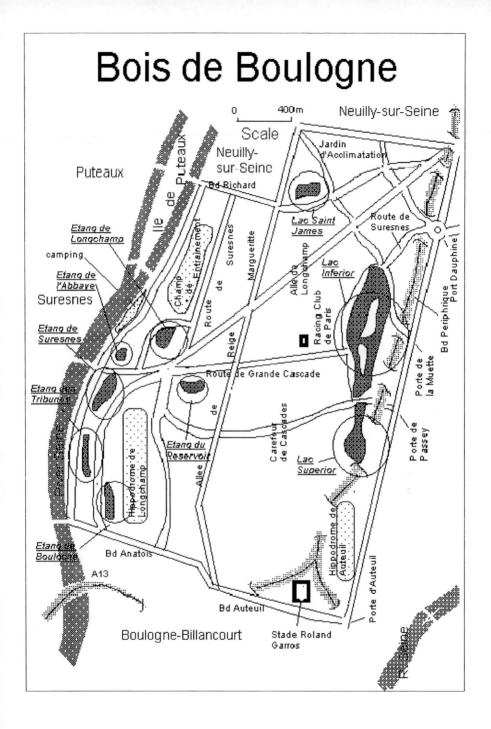

Bois de Boulogne

Lac du Reservoir, 1ha – Situated on main road through Bois de Boulogne. You can't approach by car directly since the lake is on a wooded slope. Park at the bottom. This water has a reputation for large *poisson blanc* but also contains carp, tench and bream plus a few pike and zander. It is 1.4 –2m deep. **Directions**: near *Pont de Suresnes* and Longchamp racecourse. *Carrefour de Longchamp, route de Sevres, route des Tribunes. Tram – T2 to Suresnes* and *Lonchamp. Bus – 241 – 244 – 175 – 93.*

Etang de Longchamps, 2ha – near Portes de Nueilly-sur-Seine, this is a good place for young anglers and has **disabled access**. This is a good venue for the *friture* specialist: promenaders patrol the adjacent pathways at weekends and Wednesdays. 1.2-1.8m deep, pi, za, pe, some bb, tr, p/b, barbeque area. Neighbourhood *École de Pêche* and *centre de loisirs*, for kiddies. **Directions**: car – near *plaine de bagatelle* and *Pont de Suresnes. Carrefour de Longchamp. Route de Sevres. Route des Moulins. Tram – T2 Suresnes and Longchamp. Bus – 241 – 244 – 175 – 93.*

Etang de Suresnes, 2 ha – Located by Pont de Suresnes, a good family water, it has barbeque area and the kiddies can play nearby while dad gets on with the serious business, pathway along bank. A little noisy due to proximity of the main road. A bit of a walk from the car park with all your gear. Some *silure*s present and even a Caiman crocodile! Catch zander by the submerged trees in centre of water. 1.2 - 2m deep. **Directions**: near *Pont de Suresnes* and Longchamp racecourse. *Carrefour des Tribunes. Allee du Bord de l'Eau. Route des Tribunes. Tram – T2 Suresnes and Longchamp. Bus – 241 – 244 – 175 – 93.*

Etang des Tribunes, 1ha – next door to Étang de Suresnes, barbeque area and parking up to bank. Family water, but avoid racedays because the carparks get full. 1.2 – 2m deep, za, pi, tr, ca, p/b. **Directions**: near *Pont de Suresnes* and Longchamp. *Carrefour des Tribunes. Allee du Bord de l'Eau. Route des Tribunes. Tram – T2 Suresnes and Longchamps. Tram – T2 Suresnes and Longchamp. Bus – 241 – 244- 175 – 93.*

Étang de Boulogne, 2 ha (trout fishing, requires special license) – Stocked every month September through May, 3 fish limit, wooded area, no car noise, watchout for cyclists on exit! Wire fence limits the presence of promenaders so you can cast in safety. 1.2-1.8m deep, tr, bb, pi, za.

Catch rainbow trout, brown trout and tigres, from 200gms to 2 kilos. Open except for June/July/August due to the hot weather. There are also pike, perch, black bass and stripped bass to 4 kilo (cross between black bass and *le bar*): which must only be caught using streamers. **Directions**: near *Porte d'Auteuil*: follow *boulevard Anatole France* up to river Seine then take 1st right *Stade de l'APCB parking* at end. Cross over cycle lane, lake-entrance is in front. *Metro – ligne 10, Porte de Auteuil* then take bus 241.

Étang de l'Abbaye (reserved for *Club Mouche Apnle* and *Ecole de Peche*) situated by *Pont Suresnes* and *Camping du Bois de Boulogne*.

Étangs Hauts de Seine

Regulations: no fishing after 2pm, and on Sundays and public holidays. Fish within authorised zones.

a) Parc Sceaux, 21 ha – **Gran canal**, *octagone* and **small canal**, park opening times.
b) Nanterre – **Étang du parc Matraux**, 2ha
c) Villeneuve-La-Garenne – **Étang des Hautes Bornes**, 2ha, park opening times, rods restricted to 5m in length due to overhead EDF power lines.
d) Le Plessis-Robinson – **Étang Colbert**, 2ha, park opening times.

Étangs Federaux (Meudon, Creteil, Bondy)

To view regulations – (covering depts 75-92-93-94) contact the *FPPMMA* (local angling federation), tel, 01 53141980, email: FPPMA75@club-internet.fr

a) **Étang Créteil** (42ha): (dept. 94) fish from west and south banks, depth averages 4-6 metres. Most coarse species caught here. In addition there are *silure, perche soleil* and zander. **Night fishing** for carp allowed between island and the Roseliere reserve. Allowed to **night fish** at island except for small channel separating it from the bankside. This lake is run by a division of the *Parc dept. de sports de Choisy-Le-Roi, Val-de-Marne*.

b) **Étangs de Bondy** (93), angling allowed in Étangs Isabelle, Virginie and the canal on the southern bank during opening hours of the park. Located in 4ha of parkland south of the forest between Courbon and Monfermeil. There are 5 lakes in fluvial progression. i. **Étang Dominique**, 0.2ha ii) **Etang Lawrence**, 0.2ha (stock lake-no fishing here) iii) **Étang Isabelle**, 0.5ha iv) **Étang Virginia**, 2.6ha v) **downstream canal**, 0.4ha open to angling on south bank.

Étangs de Meudon – Fôret de Meudon

4 lakes: easy access and parking. **Directions**: *RN118 or RN306. RER ligne C station Meudon-Val Fleuri.*

a) **Étang de Chalais-Meudon** – 4ha, 1-2 metres deep. Pike, zander, carp, perch and roach.
b) **Étang de la Garenne** – 1.5ha, 1-2 metres deep. Easy fish. Same species as before, plus black bass.
c) **Étang de Villebon** – 2ha, 1-2 metrs deep. Same species as above.
d) **Étang des Trivaux** – 1ha, 1-2 metres deep. Same species as above, plus black bass.

More trout fishing in Paris

Étang de 3 Sources (1.6ha): good access, open October-April - tel, 01 30751083, this is another trout lake (same regulations) located in the *dept du Val Oise by l'Isle Foret de l'Isle Adam*, 35km from Paris. **Directions**: *l'autorouteee A16, national 1, nationale 322.*

Angling clubs of Paris: *Clube de Pêche de Mouche* – www.pechemedia.com/clubmouche tel, 01 42241895. We are open to everyone from 10-12pm on Saturdays/Sundays and Mondays.

Club de Pêche aux Carnassiers – www.pechemedia.com/clubcarnassiers tel, 06 03657080, speak with Michael Pesnel

Club de Pêche a la Carpe – www.pechemedia.com/clubcarpepnle tel, 06 07397344 ask for Christian Blanquet

Le Maison de la Pêche

Opened on 12th June 1993. This purpose built angling centre was established for the protection of the environment for fisheries in Paris, it runs a multitude of angling related activities all year round and for all ages and abilities.

Situated on the Allée de Claude Monet on the, l'Ile de la Jatte surrounded by a lovely park. Its *École de Pêche* runs angling courses for children aged from 8-14 years. They run 28/4 to 30/6 and 22/9 to 8/12.

There is a fresh water aquarium containing all the types of fish you are likely to catch nearby. For school and other groups there is a visitors research centre (24 person, maximum). For further information email: mpnl@pechemedia.com

The centre is open all year, each Saturdays and Sundays from 1am-6pm, and on Wednesdays, on the 10th till 1pm and the 14th till 6pm. It is closed during August and at Christmas. The admission fee is 3.5 euros for adults and 2 euros for those 3-16 years and over 60. Groups of 5 or more are also charged 2 euros each.

On the wall hangs an antique glass case with two of the biggest catches from the River Seine that you are ever likely to see. The mirror carp weighs 37 kilos and was a world record. It was caught at l'Yonne (Dept. 77). Below, hangs a *silure,* which measures 1m 37cm in length. They can grow to over 2 metres!

Directions: It's a 10 minute walk to *Le Maison de la Pêche* from the *Metro station Pont de Levallois (entre 5 escalator).* **By car**: in Paris, leave the *Porte de Champerret,* follow the *Bd. Bineau* towards the *Pont de Courbevore.* On the, *l'Ile de la Jatte,* take a right to the *Bd. Vital Bouhot.* Park and pay, along here then walk to the *Allée Claude Monet.* **The address***: Ile de le Jatte-22, allée Claude Monet, 92300 Levallois-Peret.* Tel, 01 47 571732, fax, 01 47 580396, email: infos@maisondelapeche.net

There are lots of big *silure* specimens ready to be caught just a 5 minutes walk from some famous Parisian landmarks. One specimen to 1.88 m in length was landed at the *barrage de Suresnes.* Another hotspot is at the

Pont de Neuilly, where a 50 kilo *silure* took 30 minutes to land. There is also good general coarse angling from the barges at *L'Ile de la Jatte*.

Nicholas Vernier of PêchXtreeme runs day trips from a boat on the Pont de Levallois: meeting place is at Maison de la Peche. Tel, 01 47 571732 or email: PecheXtreeme@maisondelapeche.net

---

RIVER SAÔNE

There is public fishing along all of the banks of the river Saône. And on many of the adjoining *plan d'eaus* and *etangs*. Night fishing for carp and eels is permitted but restricted to designated areas. **Ron Woodward** has fished here many times before and has the following to say.

"The river Saône runs from north of Dijon 160km south to its confluence with the river Rhone at Lyon. It is between 200 and 400 metres wide and has a much slower current than the river Seine. Therefore, weed is often a problem later on in the year. I advise the use of braided line at these times as it cuts through well.

Common carp are the predominant species. They grow to over 30kg but are mostly caught in the lower doubles. There are bigger individual specimens in the river Seine but bigger bags are possible on the Saône due to the presence of larger shoals.

One of my favourite spots is at lovely Chalon-sur-Saône, the best swims are close to the islands and barge moorings. The *Guard de Pêche* regularly patrol these waters so make sure you are in pocession of the correct *Carte de pêche*. A mistake can cost dear in time as well as money.

Most coarse species are caught here. But the Saône is really famous for its large catfish, the *silure*. For carp fishing I usually groundbait heavily with particles (sweetcorn, hemp) adding broken down trout pellets to the mix. Tackle needs to be beefed up and expect to use strong leaders 20lb or more, to combat snags and bigger fish. Yes the *silure* are partial to a boile." Ron is more than happy to answer any questions you may have about France. Email: **Ron@catfishgroup.co.uk:**

SAÔNE AND LOIRE (71)

For angling information contact:

Fédération de Pêche de Saône-et-Loire
123, Rue de Barbenfane, BP 99
71000 Senne ce-les-Macon
tel, 03 85238300, fax, 03 85238308
email: contact@peche-saone-et-loire.org

Burgundy is a great place to start to fish the Saône-et-Loire river system. As well as the big rivers like the Saône, Loire, the rivers Seille and Doubs have great quantities of large carp exceeding 20kg in weight. The lakes are just as good e.g. la barrage da le Somme (360ha) contains carp exceeding 15-18kg. Smaller plans d'eaux like Torcy, le Breuil, Montaubry, Berthavel, *l'etang de Brandon* (45ha) and the smaller *etangs de la Bresse* and Canal de Centre all have good head of carp up to 8kg.

Silure catfish are regularly caught on the river Saône at the town of Macon to 3m in length and over 100kg in weight and also on the river Seille. Even if the numbers are less the large ones are always present. Much of the traditional pike spawning grounds have been drained for agriculture so pike numbers are down, especially on the rivers Doubs, L'Arroux and La Grosne. But sizes are up, especially on the Saône and the Seille. 70-80cm is the average length. From Chalon to Macon the carp are mainly powerful commons which are often caught close to the bank. The channel floods in spring.

Zander are regularly caught to 10kg, on La Loire, La Seille, and Le Doubs. A hotspot on La Saône is at *Darses de Chalon*, and at Macon. TheCanal du Centre has some fine zander; catch them on spinners to 2/3kg at Torcy La Somme and by Pont-du-Roi.

Black bass are found on the river Seille in excess of 2kg but less so on the river Saône. L'Arcone is good for perch. General coarse fishing is very good on the big rivers but also give it a go on the smaller, rivers Loire, L'Aronce and La Grosne. The use of *l'Anglaise* (waggler, feeder, swing tip) is ideal on the Rivers Saone and Doubs, for catching roach, bream and tench.

There is access for **disabled anglers** at l'étang de Baudurettes (6ha) and at Thil/Arroux. Here there are several special pontoons and a large area,

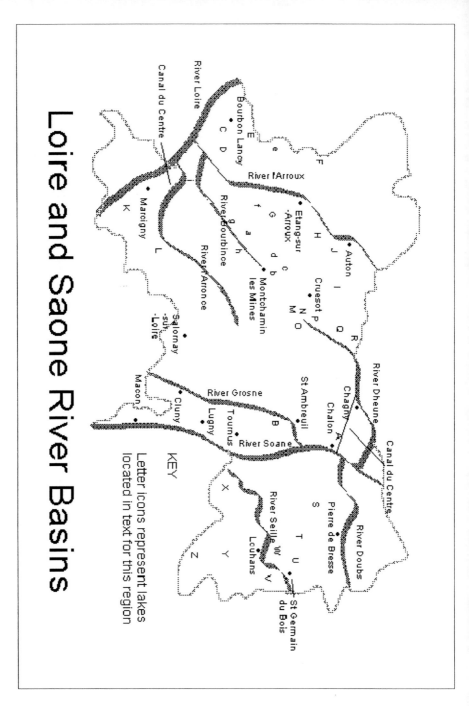

Loire and Saone River Basins

KEY

Letter icons represent lakes located in text for this region

designated for disabled anglers.

River Saône Basin

Local Angling advice: AAPPMA – Chalon-sur-Saône
Yves Soullier
8, Rue Edourd Manet
7100 Chalon-sur-Saône
tel, 03 85466799

General information: Tourisme – OT
Boulevard de la republic
Chalon-sur-Saône
Tel, 03 85483797

Accomodation: Camping de la Butte
Rue Jeen Leneveu, Chalon

A recent (August 2004) *silure* catch on the River Saône at Mâcon tipped the scales at 82kg and measured 2,24m in length, after a one hour struggle with a Monsieur Jimmy Chanussot from Sagny (71).

Zander and pike season runs from 10/5 to the last Sunday in January (pike) and last Sunday in Febuary (zander). At Llac de Pres St Jean at Chalon you can fish for pike and sturgeon, all year through. And **night fish** for carp from 1st April to 31st November.

For carp angling advice contact: Carpe Alliance
Jean Alfonso
59 Grande Rue St Cosme
71100 Chalon Sur Saône
tel, 0385484132

Or go to: The local carp group, Jean-Luc
Guillement, email: carpe71@free.fr
tel, 0385434017.

Lac de ZUP (12ha): **night fishing** permitted, max depth is 5m, some mirror carp and *amours blanc*, mostly commons, fish from right bank. The lake has mirror carp in large quantities to 22kg and *amours blanc* to

19kg. In October 2002, 900kg of carp between 5+8kg and 29 *amours* at: 7kg each were introduced into the lake by the Chalon AAPPMA.

(A) Étang de Mllart and: **Lac La Bleu** (7ha): 14m max depth, mirrors mostly, some commons, best place to fish is at top of water. **Étang de La Gaule**: at Chemforgeuil near Chalon, big density of carp makes fishing easy, there are a lot of mirrors and commons, some *amours*.

> Bouilette recipe: 500gr – flour. 200gr – corn. 200gr – soya. 50gr – caseinate. 20gr – calcium caseinate. 30gr – red Robin. 1 spoon – fruit stimulative. 2ml – banana essence. 3ml – caramel essence. 3ml – sweetcorn.

Chalon: (*AAPPMA* known as *le Gaulle de Chalonnaise*). River Saône, *domaine public, 2nd catagorie* – lots 10-16, *ibbis* 17; from PK156.5 to PK133, *Canal du Centre* lots 2,3,4 from PK 2.750 to the *32 eme écluse Mediteranee*. **Permits**: *Carte de Vacances* - 30euros. (Chalon) – Avenir Pêche, *22 Route de Lyon, Saint Remy* tel, 0385483216. *Europêche, Saint-Jean Pêche, Rue Thomas-Dumorey* (leave A7 to Chalon south) *7100 Chalon-sur-Saône*, - tel, 0385466336/0385934300

Chalon is a good choice to base a trip to the upper Saône Basin because of its location right on the river Saône. The whole department covers 110km of bank side angling. In Chalon itself there is 17km of river fishing, 10km of public banks on Canal du Centre and 100ha of plans d'eaus.

At Chalon, carp are mostly commons to modest size, they make up 90% of the catch with many reaching 9kg, but there is always the chance of a huge mirror carp, the biggest at 21.5kg. And locals do warn that *silure* will often grab your carp baits. Level concrete embankments in town offer some well-known hotspots. At *Pont Saintes-Laurent* a 20kg mirror carp was recently landed.

Night fishing permitted at Chalon lots 14-15 from PK 139 (Roy de Droux, *restaurant Ma Campagne*) to PK 145 (Canal du Centre - no night fishing here) from 1st June to 31st November.

Night fishing is permitted elsewhere on all of Chalon's AAPPMA controlled waters of the river Saône (from 1st June to 31st November) from lot 10, PK 156.5 (Gergy) to lot 17, PK 133 (ile Chaumette). All night fishing zones are well sign posted, so don't pay too much attention to *lot* nos and km markers unless you want to study a local map, or pay a visit to a French library. They are very good.

Charney-les Chalon (*AAPPMA la dorade*). River Saône, *domaine public, 2nd catagorie,*– lots 1,2,2bis,3, 4 from PK 181,800 to PK170. **Permits**: *M.Bon, Le bourg Charnay-les-Chalon* tel, 0385491285.

Creche-Sur-Saône (*AAPPMA l'arloise*). River Saône 2nd catagorie, *domaine public*, lot 35,36,37 from PK76.500 to PK69. **Permits**: *M.Monnot, Articles de Pêche* RN6, *Creches-Sur-Saône* tel, 0385371096.

Gercy (*AAPPMA La Pêche*). River Saône 2nd catagorie domaine public, lot 8+9 from PK162 to PK 136,500. North of Chalon, from Crissey to Gergy wild carp grow from 4-13kg and they offer good sport. Carp here grow over 30kg, which is exceptional for this river. **Permits**: *M.Jacolin Tabac-Journax Gercy* tel, 6385917695. **Night fishing** on River Saône, from PK162-PK164.6, clearly signposted.

Macon (*AAPPMA La parfaite*). River Saône 2nd catagorie, *domaine public* – lot 34 from PK85 to PK 76,500. From Macon south to Lyon the river Saône regains its wild banks, flowing between meadows, corn fields, forests and small hamlets. Carp here reach 20kg, 70% are commons. **Night fish** on right bank at Sance, PK83.3 – PK85.00; and at St Symphorien d'Ancelles on right bank lot no39, PK66 to PK64.7, towards the river Rhone. **Permits**: *Saône Pêche, 26 Avenue H.Herriott, Macon* tel, 0385392496.

Ormes (*AAPPMA Les Amis du port*). River Saône 2nd catagorie, *domaine public* –, lots 21+22, from PK123 to PK115. **Permits**: *M.Jarillot Marie le Bourg, Ormes* tel, 0385402523

Rivers Seille and Doubs Basin

Le Doubs is a mountain river, 430km long. Visit the stunning waterfalls at Saut du Doubs. The river Seille is 120km long. Both rivers are good for general coarse angling plus pike, zander and *silure*. The river Seille is famous for its large *silure*s and beautiful wild carp. They are difficult to catch but great fighters. **(S) Étang de la Blaude.**

Louhans offers easy access to the River Seille via a bankside track. Hard fighting common carp reach 6-15kg, there are larger mirror carp, several up to 20kg+. The river channel has a natural setting, a slow current with lilly beds and fallen trees suggesting evidence of promising swims. The fishing here in winter is good. For more information: tel, 0385753471. A **night fishing** zone is open from 1/6 – 31/10 on a stretch starting at lot 9 from the railway bridge downstream to the cut on left bank.

(T) Étang de la Tuillerie: (U) Étang Titard: (V) Étang Chauceveau: (W) Étang de St Usage: (X) Étang de Mont du Chat: (Y) Étang de la Bardlere: (Z) Étang de la Clollere.

Lac de Saint Point (400ha): Pontarlier, 2nd cat public, 4 rods, pi, za, pe, tench and some trout. 3rd largest lake in France. 40m maximum depth. It is famous for its *coregone* fish species; which originates from Switzerland. Locals fish for it from start of April and also in the autumn to November 15th. They catch them from a boat with 8/10 nymph flies dropped on a 5/6m line. Sometimes the fish go right down 40m. The best spot is upstream part of lake. Most local anglers fish l'*Anglais* style for tench and *gardons*. The best period for pike and zander is June to November, in the autumn the locals go for the big pike with colourful lures near to where the *coregone* fishermen are active. Boat hire at La Bergement-Sainte-Marie. *Tourisme*: Malbuisson tel, 0381693121.

River Grosne Basin

100 km river stretch, coarse fish downstream of the *Pont de Clermain*, upstream, it's trout only. Catch barbel on the rivers Guye, La Grande, La Grosne and parts of river Grison. Pike are caught in shallow waters of the river Grosne just before the confluence with the river Saône.
(B) Étang des Vernes.

Local Angling information:	AAPPMA
	Gilbert Touzot
	8 ruee M.Louise Zimberlan
	71250-Cluny
	tel, 03 85591725

| **General advice**: | Tourisme |
| | OT 6 Rue Merciere, Cluny |

Tel, 03 85590534

Accommodation at: Camping Municipal St-Vital
Rue des Griottons, Cluny
Tel, 03 85590834

River Dheune Basin

The river Dheune has general coarse fishing plus pike, zander and perch. There are some trout on the river Creusse at the confluence with river Dheune. The current slows up after Chagny. Fish from here: 34km to the river Saône.

(M) Reserve de Long Pedu: (N) Res de la Morte: (O) Res de Bordilly: (P) Res de Montaubry: (Q) Gravieres de Tally: (R) Étang de Bouche:

Local angling advice: AAPPMA
Jaques Bonzon
17, rue des Eglantines
71150 Chagny
tel, 03 85870430

General information: Tourisme: Syndicate d'Initiative
2, Rue des Halles, Chagny
tel, 03 85872595

Accomodation: Camping du Paquier Fane, Cagny
Tel, 03 85872142

Rivers Arronce and Sornin Basins

The river Sornin is in Beaujolais country, it is 53km long and ends at its confluence with the river Loire. Average width on its lower coarse is 10m. There is usually a strong current and it is principally a trout river. But you can fish for barbel at towns of Anguille and Lotte on the right bank, and in its tributaries.

The river Arronce has many lakes along its course. The étangs Rousset, Neuf, Comte, Grand-Landes, Loire and Broussand are all open for coarse fishing. The river has a weak current, meandering through pleasant meadows of Charollais and hedgeland farms. It is good for pike, barbel, bream, carp, roach and perch. **(L) Étang de Beaverney**.

Local angling advice:	*AAPPMA* Anzy-le-Duc Christian Cozenot Les Haines, 7110 Anzy-Le-Duc Tel, 03 85252978
General information:	Tourisme – 8, Route de Precy, Marcigny Tel, 03 85253906
Accomodation:	Camping de Charolles, Routes de Viry, Charolles Tel, 03 85240490

River Loire Basin

In all, the river Loire is 1012km in length, the longest river in France and is often 300-400 metres wide, but not here. However the current is 15 times faster than on the river Saone. The water level goes very low in summer and floods dramatically in autumn and spring. Catch carp in the calmer stretches where the current is weakest. Perch and zander are common, less so pike and *silure*. The Canal de Roanne at Digoin has a slow current and is good for perch and zander. Try also at the Loire's confluence with its smaller tributaries. **Night fishing** on river Loire at Aurilly, lots no C11, from confluence with river Urbize to *Pont de Bonnard*; and on lot no C12 from *Pont de Bonnard* to *track des Sables*.

Local angling advice:	AAPPMA Gerard Poissonnet 3, Le Coteau, 71140, Bourbon-Lancy tel, 0385892179
General information:	Tourisme Place d'Aligre, Bourbon-Lancy Tel, 0385891827

Accomodation: Camping de Saint-Prix, Bourbon-Lancy, tel, 0385891485

(C) Plan d'eau de Breuil: (D) Étang Beauchamps: (E) Étang de Oncry: (K) Étang Batardeau:

River Bourbince Basin: unfortunately the river itself is polluted at present (2004).

a) Le barrage de la Somme (360ha, plans d'eau) is well known for its massive pike towards Creusot. Where they will grow over 1.3m and weigh over 20kg. In fact 100 pike over 1m are caught here every season.

(b) Res de La Muette: (c) Lac Como: (d) Res de Montchamin: (f) Graviere des Sables: (g) Étang Clesay: (h) Étang de la Garenne: (I) Étang des Molines.

River Arroux Basin

A pleasant river in a nice setting. Variable current: with many different types of swims. From deep pools to fast shallow runs. To the south it meanders, alternating between wooded slopes and farmer's fields. The confluence with the river Loire is just downstream of Digoin. As well as usual coarse species, barbel and pike, the locals are planning to re-introduce salmon to their river.

Local angling advice: AAPPMA
Albert Milleret
La Bussiere 71550 Anost
Tel, 0385827377

General information: Tourisme
3, Avenue Charles de gaulle, Autun
tel, 0385522034

Accomodation: Camping Municipal, Alnost
Tel, 0385827907

Plan d'eau de Louvarel: at Champagnat, **night fishing** all year. **Étang de Montchanin**, *étang de la Muette*, *Lac du Plessis*, *enduros* held at these venues. **Lacs Communeaux** Laives: at Laives, 2 communal lakes, Lac no 1, lac no 2, night fishing from 1/3 – 30/11.

L'étang Bousson (42ha) is a big fish venue. At Beuvray-val-d'Arroux by Monts du Morvan the scenery is great and the carp are caught in excess of 20-30kg. **(F) Étang de Poisson: (G) Étang d'Aizy: (e) Gravieres Du Champ des Pierres.** The pike are big at the **(I) barrage du Pont du Roy** (70ha) near Epinac. **(J) Étang de Vallon:** at Autun, in 2002 5 tonnes of carp died, this disaster was due to a virus introduced by new stock and low oxygen levels after local authorities attempted to kill off algae.

SAÔNE/RHÔNE (69)

43 angling clubs make up the AAPPMA angling federation, for the Rhône region. There are 21,000 license holders who have access to 1'890km of rivers and 635ha of lakes. The AAPPMA is one of 34 federations belonging to *Club Halieutique* national organisation. A reciprocal system for fishing, different departments for south of France.

The Saône/Rhône region is divided up into the river Saône (20km stretch), river Rhône (50km stretch), Canal de Jonage (17km stretch), plan d'eau du Grande-Large, Canal de Miribel, plans d'eau du Parc de Miribal Jonage.

There are good carp at *plan d'eaus Madonne, Morment* and *Combe Gilbert* between Orlienas and Taluyers. Favourite venues for general coarse angling are *plan d'eaus Miribel Jonage* and *Le Grand Large* east of Lyon. The *étang des Dombes* has large eels.

École des Pêche: Ecôle de Pêche de Neuville-sur-Saône (including fly fishing),
M Meurier, Chemin decRoncheveux
01600 St Didier de Formans
tel, 0474003780.

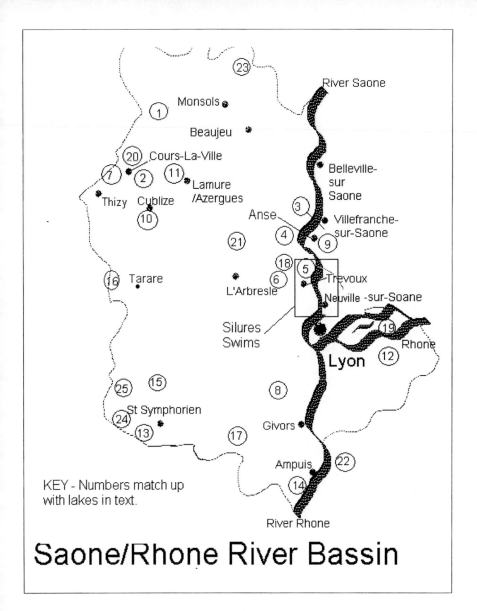

Saone/Rhône River Bassin

For all your water needs: Agence de l'Eau Rhône-Méditerranée-
Corse
2-4, allée de Lodz
69363 Lyon Cedex E7
Tél.: 04 72 71 26 00
Fax: 04 72 71 26 01

Angling in the region: Fédération du Rhône pour la Pêche
Le Norly 42 Chemin du Moulin, Carron-
69130 Ecully, tel, 04 72180180, fax, 04
78331164

Local Angling advice: Union Lyonaise des Pêcheurs a La Ligne
70, rue Pierre Corneille
69003 Lyon 3eme
Carpe de nuit (night fishing): information
tel, 04 78600730

Regulations and licenses: *Carte vacances* cost is 30 euros ($1^{st\ cat}$ waters - 1 rod, and $2^{nd\ cat}$ - 4 rods). The *Carte Journaliere* (day ticket) is available from 1/4/04 (see map for day ticket waters) it costs 6 euros and is valid only for plans d'eaux. They are open from 1st April.

Carnassiers, 2nd catagorie –pike close season, 25th January to 8th May. During this period you can still catch pike on fly. Zander close season, 29th Febuary to 8th May.

Permits: *UPL* (address given above). *Décathlon C.C. Part-Dieu, Lyon 3eme. Lyon Pêcheur, 58 Quai Piere-Scize Lyon 9eme. Canuts-Pêche 5 Rue Perrot, Lyon 4eme.*

The Saône/Rhône river system is divided into 5 key areas. Starting from north, to south, they are as follows.

1 Saône Beaujolais

2 Saône valley

The carp record for the river Saône is 26kg. Catch big bream at Neuville by the bridge and quays. And also, from the *barrage de Couzon* to the area around the footbridge de Rochetaille. Sturgeon are caught here up to 20kg. The famous *Marathon Silure* event takes place on the 26th June each year.

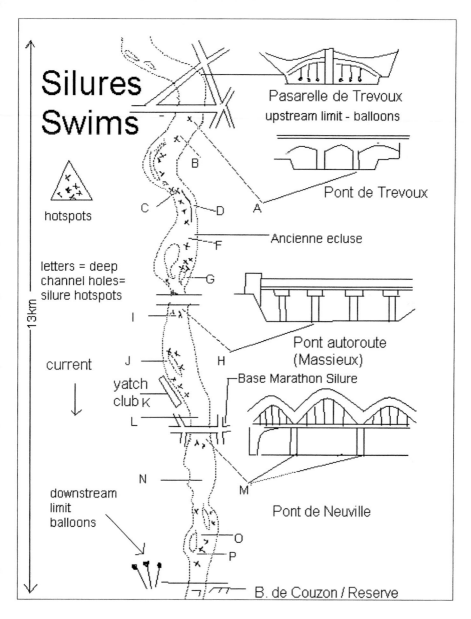

Map key, *Silure* Swims: *fosses* are holes located on the riverbed with sonar equitment by the local angling club: The prescence of which,suggest *silures* holding areas. The *fosses* are easily visible by marked buouys in the channel.

A- 10m downstream of the bridge by left support pylon. 7 metres deep.

B- Small hole upstream, of the island, 10m deep.

C- Remote and out of the way under the marker buouy. This hole is always occuppied by *silures*. 6-8m deep.

D Just downstream, on a very long bend, 9-12m deep from the barge up to the old *écluse*.

E- Hole of 12/13m depth opposite the Ski sign.

F- Hole is under the *écluse*, left bank: runs from the island up to the bridge, 8-12m deep.

G- By tree stump on left bank, a big hole, 12m deep hole running up to the bridge.

H- Hole directly in line, downstream of bridge's support pillars.

I- Upstream of the buouy, 10m deep hole, by right bank.

J- Hole is by right bank, 9/10m deep, located under buouy.

K- Hole is on long bend, right bank opposite the yatch club, outside the buouys to 9m depth.

L- no information yet?

M- Downstream of the Pont de Neuville support pilons.

N- Hole is under the buouys by left bank, rarely visited by *silures*.

O- By side of the island by right bank and downstream of this island.

P- By side of the big hole.

Neuville-sur-Saone. River Saône (8.6km stretch) downstream to the *barrage de Couzon*. Upstream to the *Pont de Massieux*. Perseverance is the key word here. It can take time to locate the nomadic shoals of carp. Heavy boat traffic doesn't put the carp off feeding. **Nightfishing**: at *Zone de Pecheurs de Fleurieu-Neuville* lot no1 both banks from PK 17,485 to PK 22.500, lot no 16 from PK 22.2 to PK 24.00 on left bank. Both banks PK 25,400 to PK 25,840, for more information contact: *Neuville de Peche* – tel, 0478981397.**Permits**: *Camping Ecluse* at Bernalin-Massicux. And at *M. Dussud, route de Trévoux a Genay, Tabac Presse*.

Local angling advice: AAPPMA Neuville-Val-Saône
                                   Salle de la Poste
                                   69250 Neuville-Sur-Saône
                                   M. Piers Meunier tel, 06 61865200
                                   Email: info@pechesaone.com

Night fishing is authorised on right bank upstream of *barrage de Couzon* (after the boundary of the reserve, sign posted), as far as the *EDF* high tension lines at the boundary of St Germain-Quinceaux (sign here also very visible). Night fishing is prohibited in an intermediate section between these two points. On the left bank upstream of the *barrage de Couzon* (after the limit of the reserve, sign posted), as far as *l'ecluse de Bernalin* at the village of Massieux. On the right bank night fishing is permitted all along between the two points. The *Pont de l'Autoroute*, right bank is downstream of *l'écluse*, so this zone is open for night fishing.

Trévoux-Quincieux, River Saone, (5.8km stretch). **(5) Le Plan de Chamalan** (2ha), day tickets available from 1/4- 31/10, za, pi, *silures*, p/b, fly fishing an option. **Permits***: Camping Trévoux. Bureau de Tabac, M. Michael Teyssier, Rue de la Commerce, Quinceaux.*

Anse (Rivers Saône and Azergues). river Saône (5km stretch). From l'Azergues, at *barrage du Pont de Morance* to the confluence with the River Saône. Day ticket waters at: **(9) Plan d'eau lieu-dit Aux Communaux** day tickets available from 1/4, all species present, **permits** from: Mme Deborne, *articles de pêche, route Nationale, Anse*. And **(4) Lac du Colombier d'Anse** tr, ca, te, pi, open from 1/1 – 31/5 Sat, Sun, and public holidays, open every day from 1/6 – 3rd Sunday in October, 2 rods, no spinning. **Permits**: *Articles de Pêche 1, Rue Georges Clemenceau, Cours-La-.Ville*

Villefranche-sur-Saone. River Saône and **(3). plan d'au de Bourdelan** (all coarse species present). This is a big reservoir of 350ha with no night fishing. Parking is by the *Presquv'ile* and by banks of the Saône. The reservoir is closed from 1st March to 2nd Friday in March. No boat fishing. Single line only from 2nd Saturday in March to beginning of pike season. Thereafter use of full complement of rods. Day tickets available from 1st April. **Night fishing** right and left banks from PK 35,700 to PK 38,500. **Permits**: *Vital* Pêche 1525 Route de Frans, Villefranche-sur-Saone, www.pechesaone.com or email: info@pechesaone.com **Permits**: Neuville Pêche, Patrick Dussud, Route Trevoux - 69730 Genay - tel, 04 78981397.

Night fishing is also permitted all year at the following sections of the river Saône. Don't worry about attempting to comprehend lot numbers and km markers, all night fishing zones are clearly sign posted.

North from Lyon: both banks from PK 6.900 to PK 15.500, PK 9.500 to PK 15.500 6km stretch, left bank only. It is 6m deep in middle of channel, the margins offer good carp habitat, shallow and weedy. Kevlar leaders are recommended to catch the big grass carp due to the presence of razor sharp zebra mussels.

Montmerle: night fishing permitted from 1st Friday of May to last Sunday in November, from Friday evening to Sunday morning. Left bank PK 52,000 to PK 54,000.

Rhône sector: Right bank of lot 11, Total service station on A7 road at Pierre-Benite, as far as *L'Auto Pont* intersection. Left bank on lot j2 from PK 8,900 to PK 14,100 (*Pont de la Sucrerie* – sugar refinery). Another spot is *Lac des Sappins*, except during the summer months.

3 Rhône Confluence

Following stocking by the local Aappma there are lots of pike over 80cm in the river Rhone around Lyon. Fish for then on the right bank upstream of *Pont Poincarre*, after where the cars emerge. Pike numbers are a little down on the River Saône because there is little ideal environment to spawn. However, some reach over 20kg in the *Plan d'eau Miribel Jonage.*

Lyon. Permits: ULPL- address shown above. *Canuts Pêche 5 Rue Perrot, Lyon 4eme. Décathlon C.C. PORT-Dieu, Lyon 3eme. Lyon Pêcheur, 58 Quai Pierre-Seize, Lyon 9eme.* **Night fishing** is permitted in all areas within city limits.

4 Canaux Rhône Nord

(12) Plan d'eau de Grand Large-Mayzieu: connects to the River Rhône via Canal de Jonage. Big mirror carp reach over 30kg, the average size is 12kg, common carp reach 17.5kg. This water has potential for bigger fish in the next few years. There are big carp present in the canal as well. Most carp at hooked at long distance of 200m or more. A boat will gain access to swims bordering the canal. The lake, bed is even but large areas of weed hinder some areas. From April through May, fish the east shore. There is **night fishing** at the campsite by the kayak and surf club. The rest of the banks are private.

Parc Nature de Iles de Miribel Jonage

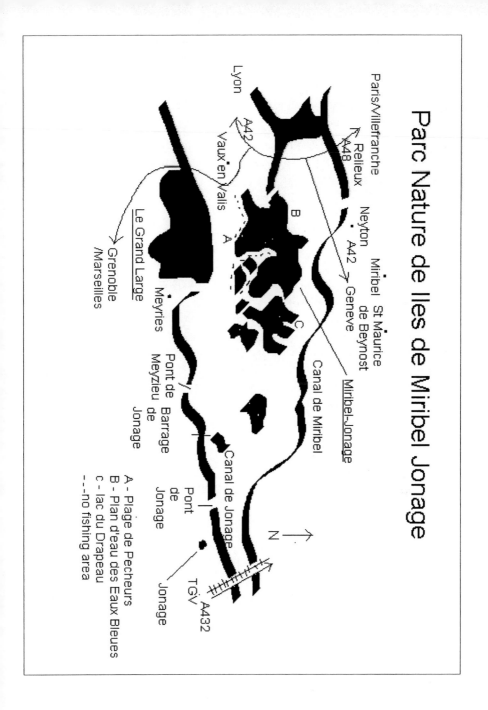

Paris/Villerfranche

Lyon

A42

Vaux en Valis

Relieux
A48

Neyton
A42

Miribel St Maurice
de Beynost

Geneve

Miribel-Jonage

B

A

C

Canal de Miribel

Le Grand Large

Meyries

Grenoble
/Marseilles

Pont de Barrage
Meyzieu de
Jonage

Canal de Jonage

Pont
de
Jonage

N →

TGV A432

A - Plage de Pecheurs
B - Plan d'eau des Eaux Bleues
c - lac du Drapeau
- - -no fishing area

32

(19) **Plan d'eau Mirbel-Jonage** (300ha) located north east of Lyon, it holds the record for largest carp caught in Rhone-Alpes region at 29.8kg many more reach at least 20kg. No night fishing at present. Nearby, fish from bank at plan d'eau des Eaux Bleues and Lac du Drapeau. (All, coarse species and black bass). Located in *Parc Nature de Îles de Miribel Jonage*. 3'000ha park, 600ha of protected areas. 230 species of birds, 30 different orchids. The sports centre *La Planete Torique* has 25 excellent sporting activities. No night fishing. No fishing from boat. **Permits**: *École de Pêche de Lyon, 70 Rue Pierre Corneille, (ULPL) 69003 Lyon* - tel, 0478600730.

Étang du Drapeau: Lyon, small lake connected to *Lac de Miribel Jonage,* lake record is 29.4kg carp caught in April 1997.

Domaine de Mepieu: at Cremieu near Lyon. Two of three lakes are for carp angling. **Le grand Étang** (50ha) is the best with carp to 20kg+ but also *silure* and grass carp. There are 10 swims for **night fishing**. The smaller **Étang de Barral** (12ha) contains 400 grass carp and carp, to smaller sizes. **Directions**: east of Lyon, *Domaine de Haute Pierre, Route de Siccieu, 38460 Cremieu* – tel, 1674907469.

5 Rhône Sud (South)

Good for pike, *silure*, eels and zander.

Givors. River Rhône (lotD4, 7.5km stretch), from Viaduc de la Mediterranee to L'Ille Barlet. And **(22) Plan d'eau –Lone du Prin**, day tickets from 1st April. **Permits**: *Tabac-Pêche 92, RN 86, Loire-sur-Rhône*, and at: *Au Pêcheurs Sportif, Articles de Pêche et Chasse, 6 rue Longarini-Givors.*

Ampuis. **(14) Plan d'eau de l'Ile de la Cheve**, pi, za, 2 rods, day tickets from 1st April. **Permits**: *Relais de Provence, M.Terpend, Ampuis* tel, 04 74561031.

More lakes for the region.

(10) Plan d'eau Lac de Cublize (40ha): aka Lac de Sappins, surrounded by forest and described by some as a truly majestic location, it is situated north west of Lyon. Avoid August and July when walkers take over. The reservoir was built in 1979, it has an average depth of 5m but reaches 15m by the dam. There are lots of carp present but few anglers bother due to difficult access to some parts of the lake. A boat is an advantage. Mirror carp in excess of 20kg. Hemp is a good bait to use because there is a dearth of roach and bream to compete with, boilies work very well. **Permits**: M.J. Gollert, *Tabac-Articles de Pêche, 15 rue de l'Hotel de Ville-Cublize.*For local information tel, 0474895283/ 0474895031.

(1) Plan d'eau Azole: **permits**: *tabac-Presse*, closed Sundays and Monday. Ca, te, tr, 2 rods, no groundbait. No spinning, day tickets from 1st April.

(2) Plan d'eau Berthier: open 1/1 – 31/5 on Saturday, Sunday and public holidays, open every day from 1/6 – 3rd Sunday in October. Tr, ca, te, pi. **Permits**: M. Bernalin, *Tabac Journaux, rue Georges Clemencau, Cours-La-Ville.*

(6) Plan d'eau Civrieaux: pi, ca, za, bb, te, 2 rods, fishing competition on 26th and 27th of April. *Ecôle de Pêche*, lessons from 6.30 – 8pm at Maison des Associations at Chazy. **Permits**: *Zoo Shop Articles de Pêche, les Arcades-Civrieux d'Azergues.*

(18) Plan d'eau Marcilly: pi, bb, ca, za, 2 rods. **Permits** from *Zoo Shop.*

(8) Plan d'eau Combe-Gibert: day tickets available from 1st April. **Permits**: *Au Pechêur Sportif Articles de Pêche 6, rue Longarini, Givors.* Day tickets for plan d'eau Madone from same shop.

(11) Plan d'eau Filatures: open 30/6 on Saturday, Sunday, Wednesday and public holidays up to 1/7 then open every day. **Permits**: *Café-Restaurant Fougerard, Le Bourg, St Vincent-de-Reims.*

(13) Plan d'eau Huronques: day tickets available from 1st April. **Permits**: Mme. M Bonnier, *Articles de Pêche, 1444, Grand Rue, St Martin-en-Haut.*

(15) Plan d'eau Jomard: ca, te, pi, no spinning, closed from 31/1 to opening date for 1st cat waters. **Permits**: *Café de lLa Gare, St-Foy-l'Argent-iere*

(16) Plan d'eau Joux: pi, p/b, tr, day tickets available from 1st April, open all year except middle of November to middle of December, 10 euros to use boat (no motors).

(20) Plan d'eau Moulin: permits from Cours la Ville. **(21) Plan d'eau Nizy**: Day tickets available from Wednesday following *Fête Nationale de la Pêche*. Closed on Tuesdays. **Permits**: *Tabac-Journaux, Place de La Liberation, Le Bois d'Oingt.*

(23) Plan d'eau Trades: no spinning, day tickets available from 1st April. **Permits**: *Café-Boulangerie* at Monsols.

(24) Plan d'eau Varagnat: ca, te, pi, no spinning, closed from 31/1 to opening date of 1st cat waters. **Permits**: *Café de La Gare, St-Foy-Largentiere.*

(7) Plan d'eau du Colombier (0.4ha):

DORDOGNE (24)

General angling advice: Fédération de La Dordogne de Pêche
16, rue des Pres – 2400 Pergueux
tel, 6553068420, fax, 0553068429
email: federation.peche24@wanadoo.fr

General information: Tourisme: 25, rue Wilson,
24009 Perqueux,Cedex.
Tel, 0553355024, fax, 0553095141.

Regulations and licenses: *Carte Vacances* – 30 euros, 4 rods. Under 16's – 14euros – no night fishing, 1 rod limit. Under 12's fish for free. 1st catagorie, pike, zander, black bass, season 13/3 – 19/9. 2nd catagorie, pike close season 25/1 – 17/4, zander –25/1 – 15/5, black bass – 25/1 – 12/6.

The river Dordogne is good to fish around St Cyprien where the varied current creates a contrasting environment of fast flowing runs and deep holes. Species present includes bream, roach, carp, pike and zander.

Dordogne
River Bassin

Marieul sur-Belle

P/d Miallet

P/d Gout Rossignol

La Coquille

River Dronne

Brantome

Riberac

Perigueux

R. Auvezere

P/d Niversac

River Isle

St Leon-sur-L'Isle

Mussidan

Etang de Forgran

Meriesplet

River Vezere

St Caprabe

Creysse

Mouleydier

Lalinde

P/d Peyrenegre

Les Eysies

Montravel

St Cyprien

Sarlat

River Dordogne

BERGERAC

La Buisson

R Dordogne

Cenac

P/d Lescarroux

Issigiac

P/d Ganne

Eymet

P/d Nette

P/d Brayssou

R Dropt

Directions: D703 St Cyprian highway towards Sarlet and Souillac to where the Dordogne flows along. Fish *l'Anglais* style for bream and roach, use a swim feeder or float. There are lots of carp over 10kg. *Tourisme*: *St Cyprien* tel, 0553303609. **Permits**: *Articles de Pêche at Sarlet* tel, 0553282659.

At Bergerac, common carp of 5-10kg are easily located, mirror carp are rarer but specimens to 20kg are present. Early season carp are concentrated in upstream areas but later on they spread out evenly throughout the channel. In summer lookout for deeper holes. Don't let the powerful current put you off just remember to beef up your tackle.

The river Isle has a great reputation for river carping, commons are plentiful in this peaceful, small, slow channel. It is usually 2-5m deep.

Étang de Grolerjac (14.5ha): located along river Dordogne a few kilometres away from Sarlet-la-Canada. At Perigord car access to all swims right up to bank: toilets and showers are provided. Good carp fishing in peaceful and secure location. Easy access by car, park by bank, toilets provided. Carp over 10kg are a common catch and there are even bigger specimens to be caught. For **more information**: *Carpe Plaisir Perigueux* – tel, 0686732559. email: pierre.navarro@wanadoo.fr

Étang de La Brâme (17ha): many carp up to 17.5kg reported catch. *Village de Pêche* at Coelacante, is a parc with 20 cottages by this commercial fishery. Big carp, *silure* and 2 sturgeon that are caught infrequently. Considered an easy fish, best swims are at peg nos 1, 2, 3, 9, 10, 11 and 12. Lake bottom is even and sandy. For **more information** contact Jean Marie at Gisale Noll – tel, 0323257746 – fax, 0323258120. Address: *route le Chateau, 12160 Villiers en Prayèrs*.

Étang de Coucon: at Hautford, carp tp 19.8kg. **Étang fédéral de Farmahaud**: at Saint-Laurent-des- Hommes, **night fishing** permitted. **Étang fédéral de Gourgousse**: at Saint-Saud Lacousiere, **night fishing** permitted.

Étang de Martine: at St Aulaye and Aubeterre. Quite well stocked with carp to 20kg, easy fishing, private water in *Floret de la Double*. It was once a carp breeding pond, there is boat hire, and a caravan with toilets and showers available, 2 rod limit.

Étang de Neuf Fonds: at Bergerac and Perigord, **night fishing**, carp to 16kg. **Plan d'Eau de Paytavit** (10ha): **Étang Fédéral de Paytavit** (10ha): **Etang Fédéral de Valjoux**: **night fishing** permitted all year. **Parc de Loisirs Vivale** (13ha): private water, fishing comes free with rent of one of the 20 holiday cottages, tel, 0553526605

AAPPMA controlled waters: **Plan d'eau Fongran** 1st catagorie water, maggots permitted, no groundbait allowed, 2 rods. **Plan d'eau Gout Rossignol** 2nd cat. **Plan d'eau Lamoura** 1st cat maggots permitted, no groundbait allowed. **Plan d'eau La Barde** 1st cat, maggots permitted, no groundbait allowed, 2 rods. **Plan d'eau La Ganne** 2nd cat. **Plan d'eau La Nette** 2nd cat. **Plan d'eau Lescourou** 2nd cat, **night fishing** at selected zones. **Plan d'eau Miallet** 1st cat. **Plan d'eau Peyrenèger** 2nd cat. **Plan d'eau St Saud** 2nd cat, **night fishing** permitted.

Private lakes: **Plan d'eau Fossemagne** 1st cat, maggots permitted, no groundbait allowed, **Plan d'eau Jumilhac1**st cat, maggots permitted, no groundbait allowed, 2 rods. **Plan d'eau La Jemaye** 2nd cat. **Plan d'eau Le Coucou** 2nd cat, **night fishing** permitted. **Plan d'eau St Estèphe** 2nd cat. **Plan d'eau Thenon** 1st cat, maggots permitted, no groundbait allowed, 2 rods. **Night fishing**: from 1/4 - 31/10

Night fishing is permitted on the following zones. All sectors are clearly signposted. Vegetable based bait products only for night fishing. 1kg of groundbait maximum.

River Dordogne: a) 100m upstream of *source de Cubertafon*, at Caudon to 100m downstream, at Vitrac.b) *Pont de Vitrac* to *Source de St Martin*, at Vitrac. c) Lot D9: *Bac d'Allas* (right bank) to upstream at first lock (right bank) 1300m to Saint Cyprien. d) Lot E2: railway bridge to *Pont routier de Trémolat* (right bank), at Tremolat. e) *Base de loisirs Laguillou* for 500m en direction de Mauzac right bank. f) 100m upstream of *Pont de St Capraise* (right bank) to 150 m upstream of *barrage de Tuilière,* at St Capraisel. g) Lot E8: 1km upstream of *Pont de Mouleydier* (right bank) at Mouleydier. h) *Promenade Pierre Loti* from access steps upstream to access stepsdownstream (right and left banks), at Bergerac. i) Lot 6: known as *port de Flaugagues* (right bank) to *Pont de Pessac* (right bank), at St Seurin Prats. j) La Mothe Montravel: 100m downstream of *le Champignon* rock to end of lot 7 at acacia trees.

River Dronne: Pont coudé (right bank) to Ecluse Moulin Grenier env.2000m, at Brantôme.

River Dropt: Pont Roman to holiday Village at Eymet.

Night fishing permitted all year round on **Plan d'eau La Gourgousse** at St Saud Laccoussiere (AAPPMA St Saud), **plan d'eau Grolejac** (except right hand shoreline), **Plan d'eau Coucon** at Hautefort, **Grand Étang les Courroux**, left bank only.

River Isle: a) *Pont du vieux bourg de Trélissac* (right bank) to *embouchure du ruisseau le Manoire* (left bank) 1000m stretch, at Boulazac. b) *Barrage des Mounards* (right bank) to *Barrage de Barnabé* (right bank), at Trelissac. c) Lot A7: 50 m downstream of *barrage des Moulineaux* (left bank) to *Pont de Gravelle* (left bank), at Razac/l'isle. d) Lot A11: Confluence of canal de St Astier (left bank) to *barrage de Crognac*, at St Astier. e) Lot A14: high tension lines (right bank) to *Pont de St Leon/l'Isle* (right bank), at St Leon/l'isle. f) Lot A16: 400 m upstream of *Pont de Planèze* (sauf reserve) *to embouchure du canal de Planèze* (right bank), at Neuvic / l'isle. g) Lot A19: 150 m downstream of Fonteyre (right bank) *to barrage de Coly Lamelette* (right bank), at Douzillac h) Lot A20: *barrage de Coly Lamelette* (left bank) to *barrage de La Caillade* (left bank), at Sourzac. i) Lot A23: *barrage de Longa* (left bank) *to barrage de St Martin L'Astier* (left bank), env 2800m, at St Medard De Mussidan. j) Lot A24: *barrage de St Martin L'Astier* (right bank) to *barrage de Chandos* (right bank), at St Martin l'Astier and St Laurent H. k) Lot A25: *passerelle du Fer* towards Cheval (right bank) to *embouchure du canal de la Filolie* (right bank) 2000m, at St Laurent H. l) Lot A28: *le Pont Cassé* (right bank) to Ruisseau Le Toulon (right bank). Lot A29: *ruisseau du Séraillé* (left bank) to *ruisseau de La Bonnette* (right bank). *Tête de l'ilot Robinson* (right bank) to Canal de Ménestérol (right bank) env 750 m stretch. Lot A29: *la rue du Chevalet* (left bank) to *ancienne papeterie (*paper factory, right bank). Lot A30: from *la tête de l'ilot des Moulineaux* for a 600 m stretch downstream (right bank). Lot A34: confluence of river Marchand (right bank) to 50 m tp downstream of *Pont de Fontrazade* (right bank). Lot A34: communal path (right bank) to *Station de pompage de M. Philippe* (right bank), all at Montpon Merestrol.

River Vezere: a) *Le pont vieux to barrage de Losse*, at Terrasson. b) *Gour d'Ariol* to Pont *de la Valade*, at Condat. c) *Pont de la Valade* to *Pont de Montignac*, at Montignac. d) Castelmerle to *Pont de St Leon / Vézère*, at St Leon / Vezere. e) *Confluence de la Beune* (left bank) to Confluence of Moulinet (left bank), at Les Eyzies. f) Brick factory to *Pont SNCF*, at St Cirq.

LOT AND GARONNE (47

Regional angling advice:	Fédération Lot et Garonne de Pêche 44, Cours du 9eme de Ligne – BP225 47006 Agen – Cedex. Tel, 0553661688, fax, 0553666892 Email: federationpeche.47@wanadoo.fr
General information:	Tourisme 4, rue Andre Chernier 4700 Agen Tel, 0553661414, fax, 6553682542

340ha of plan d'eaus 1st cat, 4000km of 2nd cat rivers, 600km of 1st cat rivers. The rivers Lot and Garonne and Canal Lateral are classed as 2nd catagorie public waters.

The Lot-et-Garonne (Dept 47) covers region of Aquitaine between Guyenne and Gascogne. The fishing takes place in an area of splendid scenery and excellent gastronomy. The riverboat trips are popular with tourists. The international mullet angling festival takes place at Agen and Passage. They catch tens of thousands.

American large mouth Black bass are caught everywhere, particularly in the canal and river Lot where fishing from a boat is an advantage in accessing those tricky swims. Casting a spinner from the bank works just as well. It's all up to the skill of the angler. Most towns along the Lot are accessible by car for the bank side. Try at Clairac or Villeneuve for a fun day out.

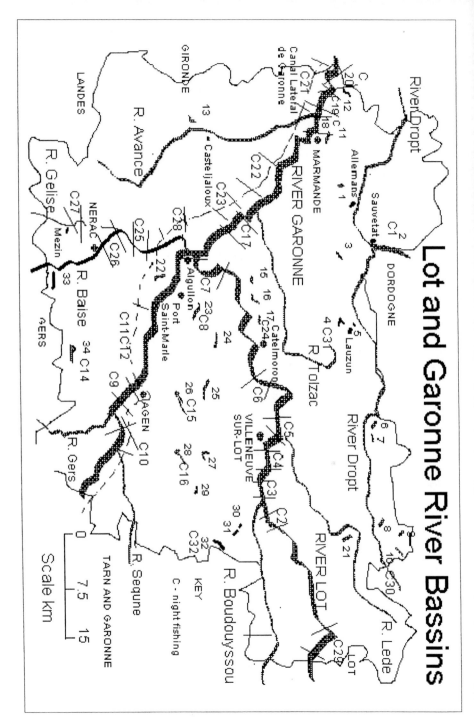

Lot and Garonne River Bassins

Scale km

0   7.5   15

41

A recommended spot is at Ste-Livrade. Every year here they hold a black bass competition. Pike and zander catches are good at Beauregard near Agen, Meilhon-sur-La-Garonne and at Aiguillon on the Lot. *Silure* reach 30kg recorded catch on the Garonne and Lot. Fish for bleak in the shallows during the evening using a fly, it's a lot of fun. Catch brown trout at Cemance and Leide (NE dept) SW depts of Ciron, Avance, Ourbise (upstream); in sandy bottomed streams amongst forest pines.

Regulations and licenses: *Carte Vacances* - 30 euros, valid from 1st June – 30th September. *Carte Journaliere* - 8 euros, valid on 1st and 2nd catagorie rivers and plan d'eaus. *Carte Jeune* – 12-16's – 12euros, 1 rod. Under 12's – 2 euros, 1 rod.

Trout season runs from 13/3 – 19/9. Pike, black bass, zander season, 1st cat waters, open 13/3 – 19/9. 2nd cat waters 8/5 - 25/1. Fishing for sea trout, salmon and sturgeon is banned.

4 rods allowed on 2nd categorie waters. 1 rod only, on 1st catagorie waters. **Tourist facilities** on Lac de Clarens at Casteljaloux, Lot and Garonne valleys, and all lakes covered by *Halieutique* (Southern France angling federation collective).

Night fishing: permitted between 8/5 – 1/11 on 2nd catagorie waters only. Except at zone 2 of La Garonne, (basin 1), 15/7 – 1/11. Numbers, and letter C before each lake mentioned corresponds with their location on the sketch map.

La Vallee de la Baise-Gelise: L'Abret en Gascogne. The river offers great potential for tourists and anglers alike. The river Gelise is famous for its pike on downstream stretches.

Plan d'eaus 2nd cat public at: 33- **Villeneuve-de-Mézin** (18ha): ga, ca. **Night fishing** is permitted at two spots on the river Baise: **C25**. Between *l'ecluse de Narac* and *l'ecluse Bapaume* for a 1.250km stretch. **C9**. From *Pont de Bordes* (limit of domaine public) to *barrage de Saint-Leger* for a 14km stretch. One on the Gelise: **C11**. From *Pont du CD 656* at Mezin to *Moulin de Courbian* for a 2.2km stretch. And one on the Canal Lateral: **C28**. From *Pont de Buzet* at *l'ecluse no 42 de la Gaule* at villeton for 11.8km stretch, this section joins up with **C18**. at Garonne basin 2. **Permits**: *Maison de la Presse, Place de l'Eglise – 47170 Mezin.*

La Vallee du Dropt: vineyards dominate the horizon of *le Pays de Duras aux ports de Perigord.* Upstream Dropt is famous for its *gougon.* Downstream is good for pike, zander and black bass. Tench and carp are present here. Fish for rainbow trout on tributaries of the Dropt from mid March to end of May. The river Dourdenne is good for pike and black bass.

Plan d'eaus 2nd cat public at: 1-**Terme-Gros** (7ha): ca, ga, pi. 3-**Saint-du-Loup** (12ha): ca. 5-**Lauzun** (1ha) ga, ca, pi, pe, tr. 6-**Queille** (6ha): ca, pi, za, ga. 7-**Nette** (27ha): ga, pi, za, pe, ca. 8-**Pesquiè** (3ha): za, ca, tr. 9-**Ganne** (35ha): pi, ca. **Night fishing** on 3 carp lakes at: **C1** 2-**lac du Lescouroux** (112ha): night fishing from 500m upstream of dam, right bank, open from 3rd Saturday in May, za, ca, boats permitted. **C31** 4-**lac des Graoussttes** (36ha): night fishing at St Colomb-de-Lauzon. **C30** 10-**lac du Brayssou** (56ha): pi, ga, ca. **Permits**: *Tabac-Presse, Avenue de Gramont, Sauvetat du Dropt.*

La Vallee de La Garonne, (basin 2): *le Pays du Marmandais* between Guyenne and Garonne. Boat day trips on La Garonne are popular with visitors and a good way to rec the river. The river Garonne's reputation is built on its populations of pike, zander and *silure.* The carp and barbel fishing is just as good. In spring, catch trout from the forest streams of the Landes region.

Plan d'eaus 2nd cat public at: 13-**Clarens** (21ha): ga, tr, pi, za. 18-**Magre** (4ha): ca, za, ga.

There are four locations on the river Garonne where **night fishing** is permitted. **C17.** 1.7km stretch from *l'embouchure du ruisseau du Caillou* to *l'embouchure de l'Ourbise.* **C18.** From *Pont de Pierre de Marmande* (PK86) to *Pont de chemin de Fer* (iron bridge) (PK88), for a 2km stretch. **C19.** 3.2km stretch from *Pont de Couthures* to *l'embouchure du risseau de la Gupie.* **C20.** From *l'embouchure du risseau le Tord* (Meilhan-sur-Garonne) (PK100.7) for 300m downstream (PK101), left bank only. The Canal Lateral is worth a go and offers 4 **night fishing** locations at: **C23.** From *Pont de Buzet* (Basin de Braise) to *l'ecluse no 42 de la Gaule*, an 11.849km stretch. **C28.** From *l'ecluse no 42 de la Gaule* at Villeton, for 11.849km stretch. **C22.** From *Pont de Fourques* to *l'ecluse no 45*, known as *l'Avance*, at Montpouillan, downstream for a 3.527km stretch. **C21.** From l'ecluse no 47, known as *des gravieres*, at Meilhan, to *l'aqueduc* *du Lisos* (dpt. limit) for a 3.644km stretch. **C29.** 11-Lac de Marachaux (4ha): ga, ca, at St-Bazeille. **C30.** 12-Lac de Beaupuy (5ha): ca, pi, ga, night fishing. **C24.** Lac de Loparde. **Permits**: *Pêche-Chasse, RN 113 – 47200 Marmande.*

La Vallee de La Garonne, (basin 1), l'Agenais. 2nd cat. Rivers are rich with pike, zander, *silure* and black bass. Also carp and barbel. There are 2 **night fishing** spots, on La Garonne and on Canal Lateral (aka Canal de Garonne) for 17km, indicated by signposts. The tributaries offer good coarse sport. Le Gers contains zander and pike.

Plan d'eaus 2nd cat public at: 14-**Damazan** (6ha); ga, ca, pi. 22-**Touret** (4ha): ga, pe, ca. 25-**Néguenou** (12ha): ga, ca. 27-**Monbalen** (6ha): ga, pi, za, ca, tr. 29- **Laroque-Timbaut** (1ha): trout lake – no kill, open from November through mid March. 34a-Lac des 3 Chênes (1ha): tr, ga,

Night fishing at: **C10**. From *Pont du L'Ayrac* (PK11.500) to *barrage de Beauregard* (PK16.875), along a 5.375km stretch. **C9**. From *Pont de Pierre*, d'Agen-le-Passage, (PK19) to *Pont Canal* Agen-le-Passage, (PK20.500), for a 1.5km stretch. **C11**. On Canal Latéral: a 17.131km stretch from *Pont de Pourret* up to *Pont de Sérignac*. **C15**. 26-Lac de Talives (16ha): ga, ca, pi, za, 2km stretch upstream of reserve, right bank. **C16**. 28-Lac de Bajamont (24ha): ga, pi, pe, ca, tr. **C14**. 34-Lac de Lamontjoie (15ha): right bank only, ga, ca, pi, za. **Permits**: *Au Royaume de la Pêche, 7 Place Peleton, 4700 Agen.*

La Valle du Lot: confluence with river Quercy. Good for pike, zander, black bass and *silures*, in the larger rivers. Especially in deep holes on the Lot. Carp fishing is good on the Lot, where you will catch mostly pristine common carp up to 12kg on a frequent basis, especially in the lower stretches. The river Lot has lots of *silures* over 52 kg and 2m long. The pike record for this river is 13kg, and 1m 15cm long. The canal has the biggest perch, at 1.75kg and 47cm long, the zander record stands at 11.5kg, black bass at 2kg, 51cm long, and the carp record is 22kg, 1m long.

Plan d'eaus, 2nd cat public at: 15-**Latapie** (6ha): pi, ca, za. 16-**Montarbat** (3ha): bb, ga, ca. 17-**Laparade-Feytous** (5ha): ca, pi, za. 17a-**Charlotte** (22ha): pi, ca. 17b-**Pradignas** (8ha): pi, ca, za. 17c-**Platan** (4ha): pi, za, ca.19-**Lacombe** (6ha): bb, ga, ca, tr. 20-**Lande basse** (7ha): ca. 21-**Monflaquin** (3ha): ga, ca, pi. 24-**St-Sardos** (17ha): ca. 30-**Labarthe-bas** (7ha): tr, pi, za, ca. 31- **Labarthe-haut** (3ha): trout lake – no kill, open all year.

Night fishing on the Lot: **C29**. *Pont de Condet* (PK 80,8500 to *Pont de Fumel* (PK 78,500), for a 2.350km stretch. **C2**. *L'embouchure du ruisseau* St Germain (PK55.7500) to the airfield (PK 54.6) 1.150km stretch. **C3**. *L'embouchure du Bouydoussou* (PK59) to pumping station (PK60) for a 1km stretch. **C4**. From moulin de Gajae (PK50.4500 to *Pont de Bastérou* (PK49.7500), for a 700m stretch. **C5**. From Pont de Casseneuil (PK39.375) to 1km downstream of (PK38.375). **C6**. From *Pont de Sainte-Livrade* (PK31.350), 800m upstream to (PK32.150). **C7**. *L'embouchure du Chautard* (at Bourran) (PK6.750) to *barrage d'Aiguillon* (PK2.750) for a 4km stretch. **C8**. 23-Lac de Canet at Galapian (20ha): ca, ab, pe, pi. **C32**. 32-Lac de Riconne (17ha): ca, pi, at Penne-d'Agenais. **Permits**: Boulangerie, Bureau de Tabac-Presse, 47320 Lafitte-Sur-Lot. And at: *Articles de Pêche 15, Rue da la Convention – 47300 Villeneuve-sur-Lot.*

TARN AND GARONNE (82)

Regional angling advice:　　Fédération du Tarn-et-Garonne Pêche (82)
275, avenue de Beausoleil
82000 Montauban
tel, 0563630177, fax, 0563630920
email: fedpeche82@nerim.net

4,000km of rivers, plus 112km of streams and lakes, and 1150ha of plan d'eau all 2nd catagorie public (public fishing areas). The rivers Garonne, Tarn and Aveyron are classified as 2nd catagorie public waters.

General information:　　Tourisme
B.P. 534 – 82005 Montauban Cedex,
tel, 0563217909, fax, 0563668036,
email: cdt82@wanadoo.fr

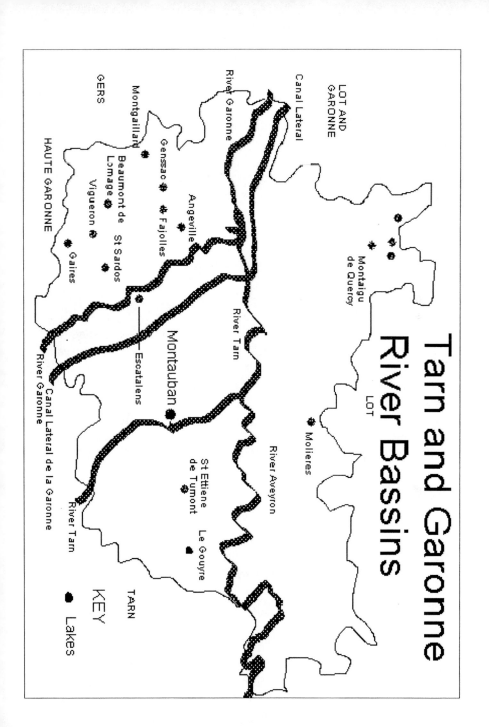

Tarn and Garonne
River Bassins

LOT AND GARONNE

GERS

HAUTE GARONNE

River Garonne

Canal Lateral

Montgaillard

Genssac

Beaumont de Lomage

Vigueron

St Sardos

Fajolles

Angeville

Gaires

Escatalens

Montauban

River Tarn

Canal Lateral de la Garonne
River Garonne

Montaigu de Quercy

LOT

Molieres

River Aveyron

St Ettiene de Turmont

River Tarn

Le Gouyre

TARN

KEY

● Lakes

46

Fish a 20km stretch of river Tarn between Lafranchaise and Moissac. Over the last 3 years this has become a good carp venue. Downstream from Montauban after the confluence with the river Aveyron, on lower stretches, the Tarn takes the form of a slow and powerful river. Meandering between orchards, it passes Lafranchaise then Mossaic and ends up at its confluence with the Garonne after the plan d'eau St Nicholas de la Grave.

Over this stretch the river Tarn is a broad 100-200m channel and rather deep, 4/5m average, with deeper holes to 10m depth. The current is quite slow here due to the influence of a number of small dams. The riverbed is principally made up of pebbles with a bed of silt deposited towards the bank in slacker water. In spite of the increase in the number of anglers, angling pressure remains light, as it does at St. Nicholas de la Grave reservoir.

The largest carp in the river Tarn are mirrors over 20kg, especially in the downstream part of this stretch and also close to the confluence with the river Garonne. The Tarn carp record is currently 23kg. However, it is the indigenous common carp that prevails. Although generally smaller at 6-8kg average weight, they do reach 10/15kg on occasions. Nevertheless, they are great fighters "pound for pound" and are easily capable of shredding cheap mustard hooks, so use raptors. Big leather and mirror carp are also present but in much reduced numbers. Expect lots of runs both day and night from the numerous superior swims, remember that the banks are often overgrown.

The river Tarn has also has a good head of zander, pike, black bass and bream skimmers. This stretch is a 2nd catagorie public water, boat fishing is permitted here. For night fishing contact the local angling federation tel, 0563630177. **Tourisme**: 0563040185. A word of warning, due to the high density of *silures*, avoid using meat based boilies and pellets.

Accomodation:	L'Ille du Bidounet ***campisite on the banks of the Tarn near Moissac, and is an ideal spot for carpists. Night fishing is permitted. It's open from 1st April-30th September. There is **disabled access** and the camping represents good value at 11 euros per day.

Useful information: including night fishing reservations	Service Departemental de Reservation Loisirs accueil Tarn et Garonne (local govt office), 7, bd Midi-Pyrenees – 8200 Montauban – tel, 0563217961 – fax, 0563668036 email: loisirs.accueil82@wanadoo.fr or go to: http://www.resinfrance.com./tarn-et-garonne/

Regulations and licenses: the *Carte de Vacances* costs 30 euros and is valid from 1st June -30th September. Under 16's: *Carte Jeune* costs 24euros. 4 rod limit on 2nd cat waters. Pike close season runs from 25th January to1^{st} March. Zander close season is from 31st December to 8th May.

École de Pêche:	Montabeau, M. Delcros, tel, 0563032565, it's open every Saturday from 2pm till 5pm from March through June and again from September through November, at the local canal.
	Fête de Pêche is on $5^{th}/6^{th}$ June in Montabeau. Open to everyone.

For information about where it's possible to use a boat contact:	*D.D.E.* (service CHAC) tel, 0563222363. Boats (motorised) are permitted on the rivers Tarn and Garonne, 5kph speed limit and not nearer than 30m of the bank. No boats are allowed on the river Aveyron. On private lakes it is left to the owner's discretion. In general they only allow rowing boats.

Lac de St Nicholas de la Grave (400ha) is situated on the Tarn at its confluence with the river Garonne. This is a virgin location, with a massive stock of superb carp, the fish fight harder than seems possible and are spread evenly across the water. The lake has 50km of banks. Boats permitted. There are carp here whose average weight is 8-10kg.

Many reach 15-17kg and often over 20kg. Specimens in excess of 30kg have been sighted. Over 48 hours, 15 teams of French anglers caught nearly 600kg of carp in a recent *enduro*. Many swims can only be accessed by boat and for this reason have rarely been fished. The enormous potential of this venue has yet to be realised. It is 4m deep at upstream, 10m deep by the dam. **Night fishing** is permitted in 3 zones, 6km of shoreline in total. **Directions**: right bank of water is accessed by RN113, from Moissac, and on left bank by RD15.

Fish species found in Garonne-Tarn: pike- introduced legally in the 1960's by the local angling federation into the river Rouergue and all channels of the river Aveyron, Lot and tarn. The best specimens are located *in Lacs de Saint-Geniez d'Olt, Castelnau-Lassot, La Creoux and Golinhac*. Newer populations can be found at Pont de Salors and Pareloup. See Aveyron section for more information on these waters.

Zander to 5kg are easily caught at Rouergue. *Vandoise* is the predominant species, they grow to 2/3kg but usually to 1kg.. They prefer the faster current in summer and deep slow water in winter (don't we all). Tench grow to 3kg. The Carp record is 28kg caught at Lac Saint Geniez. Barbel are caught everywhere but especially in upstream channels. They reach 6kg on the rivers Tarn and Lot. *L'Ombre* is caught on fly in fast water.

Plan d'eaus 2nd cat public (no day ticket required): Lac de Font Bouysse: at Montaigu-de-Quercy: **night fishing** on *lac de Fontbouysse. Le Tordre. Le Gouye. Escataens. Cordes Tolsannes. Angeville. Fajolles. Gensac. Montgaillard.*

Lac de Beaumont De-Lomagne (30ha): A beautiful private water with good fishing sport. The average depth is 4m, there are many carp from 25kg up to 28.30kg, there is good car access to the majority of swims, but remember to use the car park after unloading. **night fishing** at *plan d'eau communal*, 2000 m stretch beginning at *la plage* and the *gîtes*. 22 swims, open for the months of July and August, 20 anglers maximum. **Permits:** Brigitte LeFreure- tel, 0565261200 and *Camping du Lac* – tel, 1663652643. Vigueron Garies*, Base de Loisir*: at St-Sardot and Sardos.

Plan d'eaus 2nd cat prive (day ticket): Caussade Monteils: ***Plan d'eau du Parc de la Lère***. At Saint-Beauzeil: ***Plan d'eau de Saint-Beauzeil*. Plan** *d'eau de Pratgraussais* at Albi, **disabled access**, catch big *silures* at this location. *Les plan d'eau*: at Le Pas des Betes, **night fishing** zone near dam.

Lac de Fourrieres: at Caselsarrasin, situated on the river Garonne just prior to the river Tarn confluence. It has massive potential for big carp. At present they are not that big. At Baise by the river Garonne there are several gravel pits which hold good carp. **Lac de Parisot**: at Perigueux, in a 2002 enduro one day event three carp were caught weighing 15.7kg, 16.5kg, and 22kg. The average weight of fish caught that day was 14kg.

Night fishing zones on the Garonne and Tarn. Use vegetable based bait products only, at night. Display a nite lite.

River Aveyron: **Albias**: 300 m stretch from, left bank of *l'embouchure* (upstream) *de la Mouline* to the river Brive (downstream). Bioule: right bank, 600 m stretch from *l'embouchure* of river Rioumet (upstream) to the pumping station du Bridou (downstream).

Négrepelisse: left bank, 700 m stretch from *Pont de Bioule* (upstream) to the pumping station called M. Fraciel.

Saint-Antonin: right bank, from the old abbettoir (upstream) to 50 m upstream of Roumégous mill (downstream)

River Garonne: Castelsarrasin - St Nicholas: right bank, 3000 m stretch beginning at Métairie-Haute (upstream) to the confluence of Tarn (downstream).

Castel Mayran-Castelsarrasin: right bank, 2000 m stretch from the *Pont de l'autoroute* (upstream) to the right of the gravel pit *RUP*.

Saint-Nicolas de la Grave: left bank on a stretch 850 m downstream of the source du Canal de collature (upstream limit) to 750 m upstream of the same canal (downstream limit). And left bank, from 300 m upstream of *Pont Coudol* (upstream) to 400 m downstream of the same bridge.

Auvillar, Espalais, Saint Loup and **Valence d'Agen**: both banks, 2000 m stretch from *Pont d'Auviller* (upstream) to the *Pont de Mondou* (downstream).

River Tarn: **Labastide Saint-Pierre**: left bank, 3500m stretch from *Pont de Reynies* (upstream) to the mill (downstream).

Lafrançaise: left bank, 1100 m stretch from the *Pont du Saula* (upstream) to 50 m upstream of barrage de Rivière basse (downstream). Lafrançaise: right bank, 1010 m stretch beginning 660 m upstream of river Nauze to 350 m downstream of same river.

Lafrançaise: right bank, 1350 m stretch fromCantou (upstream) to the *Pont du Saula* (downstream). Lafrançaise, Lizac, Les Barthes, Labastide-du-Temple: both banks, 4000 m stretch from Brugau (upstream) to 50m upstream of *barrage de Ste Livrade* (downstream).

Moissac: left bank, from *Pont Napoléon* (upstream) to the confluence with the Garonne (downstream). Moissac: right bank, 1000 m stretch starting 50m upstream of *la digue goudronnée* (upstream) to the confluence with the *canal de collature EDF* (downstream).

Montauban: both banks, from 50 m downstream of barrage de Corbarieu (upstream limit) to 50 m upstream of *barrage de Lagarde* (downstream limit), with the exception of 50 m either side of the barrages.

Villebrunie -Nohic-Orgueil-Reyniès: from boudary with département de la Haute-Garonne (upstream limit) to 50 m upstream of *barrage de Lamothe-Saliens* (downstream limit), with the exception of 50 m either side of the barrages.

And at **Roque-Courbe** there is **disabled access** and **night fishing** (R Tarn).

Sturgeon are the kings of the rivers Loire, Garonne, Rhone and a few others. French annual production of caviar from the Gironde estuary (European common sturgeon) was 5-10 tons in 1920's and 1930's. Esturion numbers fell to 4'000 due to over fishing, pollution, and loss of habitat. Fishing for them was banned in 1982. However, annual *Baeri esturion* production remains at 1 ton.

Beluga caviar sells for 3'000 euros per kilo on the French market. Transmontas and Beari caviar sells for 1'000 euros per kilo. Annual world production of caviar fell from 8140 tons in 1997 to just 150 tons in 2001!

The common sturgeon grows to 3.5m and weighs up to 300kg. One of the largest, was caught in the River Thames, it weighed 350kg. They usually go up the Gironde in April/March, May/June is spawning time on gravel beds in deep water. The young are born in brackish water of the estuaries.

Siberian sturgeon are present in *etang Montpon* in Aquitaine and at *lac de Curton* (33). For sports fishing, smaller specimens are present between 15+30kg at Cheffes on the river Sarthe in north Angers (49).. One was caught recently to 21kg in 1998. Two species can be fished from still water. The Beari, and Transmontas. They will eat, everything in the lake, boiles work well. During a fight they will leap straight out of the water, just like Irish pike They will fight harder than carp so beef up your tackle.

AVEYRON (12)

Regional angling information: Fédération de lAveyron de Pêche
Moulin de la Gascaire BP 305
12003 Rodez, cedex
Tel, 0565684152 fax, 0565685020
email: FEDERATION.PECHE.12@wanadoo.fr
www.pecheaveyron.com

General information: Tourisme de Aveyron
17, rue Aristide-Briand – BP831
12008 Rodez, cedex
Tel, 0565755570 fax, 0565755571

École de Pêche: *Ecôle de Pêche*: de vallee du Tarn tel,
0670022240, Aveyron tel, 0565684152,
Villefranchois tel, 0565451839.

Fishing guides – Bruno tel, 0565755570, email:
s/a.aveyron@wanadoo.fr

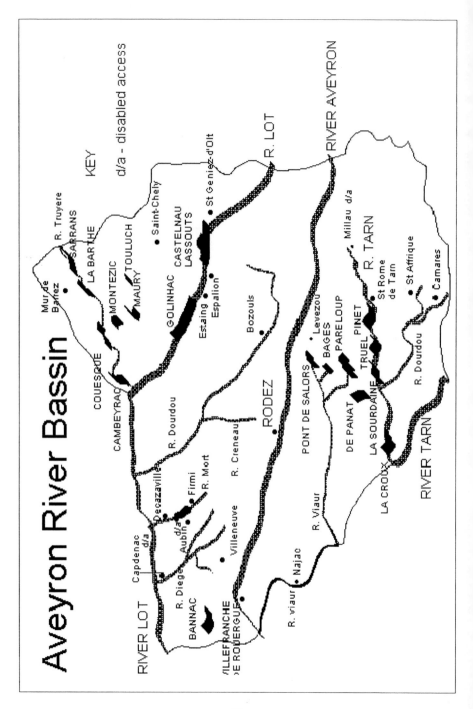

Aveyron River Bassin

KEY

d/a - disabled access

RIVER LOT

R. LOT

RIVER AVEYRON

RIVER TARN

R. TARN

Mur de Barez

R. Truyere

SARRANS

LA BARTHE

TOULUCH

MONTEZIC

MAURY

Saint-Chely

GOLINHAC

CASTELNAU LASSOUTS

St Geniez-d'Olt

COUESQUE

Espalion

Estaing

Bozouls

CAMBEYRAC

R. Dourdou

Decazaville

Firmi

R. Mort

Aubin

d/a

R. Creneau

Villeneuve

RODEZ

PONT DE SALORS

Levezou

BAGES

PARELOUP

DE PANAT

TRUEL PINET

Millau d/a

St Rome de Tarn

St Affrique

Camares

R. Dourdou

LA SOURDAINE

LA CROUX

Capdenac d/a

R. Diege

BANNAC

VILLEFRANCHE DE ROUERGUE

R. Viaur

R. viaur

Najac

6,500km of 1st cat rivers, 150ha of 1st cat lakes and reservoirs, 500km of 2nd cat rivers, 4025ha of 2nd cat lakes and reservoirs

Some of the best carp fishing in France is found in the lakes of the Aveyron region. The top caught weight reaches 28kg. **Lac du Levezou** (25km S/W of Rodez) is good for carp, fish at the intersection of its three arms, where you will locate a gently sloping bank. Look into the water, rocks on the bottom indicate the presence of crayfish, a carp food source.

Nightfishing is permitted all year at the following venues, signs indicate where to fish. Baits restricted to vegetable based at night.

1. River Lot
2. River Aveyron ar Najac
3. Lac de Pinet, Disabled access at St Rome-de-Tarn
4. Lac de Pareloup: whole reservoir.
5. Lac de Sarrans: whole water.

Licenses: *Carte Vacances* valid from 1st June – 30th September, *cartejeune* valid for under 16's cost 8 euros, for under 12's cost is 2 euros, valid for 2nd cat. waters only and 1 rod. *Carte Journaliere* valid on all 2nd cat. rivers and 1st and 2nd cat. plan d'eaus. *Carte Journaliere* only permitted on 2nd cat. rivers but allowed on 1st and 2nd cat *plan d'eaus.*

Regulations: 1st cat. waters open 13/3 – 19/9, 2 rod limit in lacs de retenue Edf, Bages, Goul and Gourade. No maggots on 1st cat. waters, but grounbait is tolerated on the following waters: a) river Aveyron upstream of pont de Montrozier b) River Tarn downstream of pont de Paulles. c) River Sorgues downstream of Truans highway at St. Affrique d) On the lakes EDF, of Goul, Gourde, Bages: hook bait only permitted, no groundbait. Trolling from a boat is banned.

Trout: on La Jonte, Le Tarn, Le Cernon, Le Dourdou de Cameres, La Sourgivs, La Dourbie and Le Durzon, 20cm minimum size, 10 fish limit on 1st cat. waters.

Reserves de Pêche are no fishing areas created especially for hatcheries and nurseries. They are marked by, easily spotted signs. If you are in doubt tel, 0565684152.

2nd cat. waters, 4 rod limit. Pike close season 26/1 – 7/5. Zander close season 5/4 – 11/6. No fishing for Black bass on *lac de Pont de Salors* and regulated fishing on *lac du Moulin de Bannec*.

River Aveyron: sections of fast current interupted by a series of wide deep pools where the flow is almost motionless. You can fish all along its length despite some short fast stretches. The river is split into two sections, which have completely contrasting natures. Upstream of Rodez it flows through a flat broad plain bordered by grazing pastures, very pastoral. Recently the channel has been cleaned up and the banks have now returned to their lovely natural state. Downstream of Rodez the terrain becomes undulated; wooded hills command the high ground. In spite of the broken releif access points are often and easy. Considerable financial effort has been made to purify the river water of the river Aveyron, especially around Rodez. The situation has now improved considerably of late. The main tributaries are good for trout fishing. **Night fishing** from: *Pont de Blasé* to Cantagrel highway at Najac.

The **River Dourdo de Cameres**: not to be confused with the river Dourdo de Conques further north. This is a large, beautiful river full of fish set in a boxed valley that is skirted permantely by a network of roads making for easy access and lots of parking areas. When it rains hard the clear water turns to a red/chesnut colour, returning to normal after 10 days. The upstream section is mainly a trout fishery but because it's so nice you might like to investigate. 2nd catagory water starts from *Pont de La Boriette*, 3km below Camares. Here the channel is a broad powerful current as it passes by Mountlaur and vabres-l'Abbaye. To slightly downstream of Saint Affrique it is joined by the splendid river Sargues. From here on the channel forms broad meanders bordered by poplars, there after its current dies in gravel pits. After 15km it is joined by the river Len, and soon after journey's end is at the confluence with the river Tarn.

River Tarn: this is a super river, quite large and characterised by its blue water, so clear that you can count the pebbles on the riverbed. Its tributary, the river Rance is one of the most beautiful in the region. The main tourist attraction is the surrounding limestone cliffs and caves of Causses which gives the eastern upstream part of the Tarn its exceptional water quality that is perfectly suited to the trout's environment i.e. tepid and clear. There is **disabled access** for anglers at Millau. There is a lot of coarse fishing, downstream from Saint-Rome-de-Tarn where, it flows into four reservoirs of the EDF (*Electricity de France*); Pinet, le Truel, La Jourdaine and La Croux.

The lakes of Aveyron region are largely composed of reservoirs. Some are set in valleys with so precipitous a gradient that access to them becomes the preserve of local fishermen with the *savoir-faire* to traverse their steep banks. Others, those included here give you moderate to very good access, depending on location. Some lakes are best fished from a boat for accessing those hard to reach swims, this doesn't mean you can't fish from the bank. Other lakes ban boats altogether. Many have good family based leisure facilities.

Be careful as the banks of some resevoirs suffer from erosion due to the changing water levels as a result of regular dam activity.

Lac de Bage: tr, p/b, pe, ca, te, no water sports means that this is a peaceful spot. The water quality is good and clear, access to the banks is good, few pike and zander, most fish for trout. Good spot is 4km stretch of Bages stream (south east shore), and on jetty left of Trappes (east shore). **Directions**: half of lake, dam end is accessed by easy dirt track. To access, areas around Trappes and Intrans (sout west shore), follow farm track. A good place for trout is 2km up Bages stream where it joins La Viaur stream but it's a bit overgrown.

Barrage de Cambeyrac (26ha): tr, p/b, pi, ca. Located in a shallow, pleasant valley, the water is 5km long and 100m wide. It has two feeder streams, Le Goul (top of lake) and Le Selves (east shore). As a whole, the lake is quite shallow and is subject to a change in the water level of up to 2m due to HEP activity. The best places to fish are downstream between the *passarelle* (footbridge) and the dam. **Directions**: Drive around lake by following *route d'Entreygues* (dam end) to Covesque (north end of water) on right bank, and ¾ of left bank by *route de Campouriez* (east shore). Access is better on right side where there are sandy shallow inclined banks that alternate with steep tree lined shore.

Barrage de Castelnau-Lassouts (218ha): aka lac de Saint-Geniez, at St Geniez d'Olt, p/b, pi, za, pe, ca, ba. A 25km long (200m-400m wide) thin reservoir in the Lot basin, with 3 tributaries, le Mousseau, le Roudil, le Merdanson. One of the most beautiful lakes you will ever visit, it draws carp anglers from all over Europe attracted by its hard fighting fish. Carp average 12-13kg, the biggest common go to 25-28kg, the lake record is 32.5kg! It is very low in autumn, but full in spring and early summer. During the night the water level can rise one metre under heavy rain so **be careful**.

The pike and zander feed well on the huge amount of *poisson blanc* in the lake. Fishing from the boat is popular, but for the best spots from the bank just ask at one of the nearby hotels or tackle shops. Most of the shoreline is steep and covered in dense undergrowth. But it's possible to fish from the bank. **Directions**: access is best at top and bottom of reservoir. a) From St Geniez (bottom of lake), right bank the road follows the shoreline towards Lous on the left bank, where you arrive there afterwards at Cabanc, here there are boat ramps and jetties to fish from. Finally, starting from the 2 dams at the top of the lake, go on foot to locate swims on either bank. Deadbaiting, here or spinning is the way to go for that elusive carnivor. Boat hire available. You are encouraged by the Guide to change swims if blanking. This is definitely a lake for the dedicated carp fisherman.

Maurice's Campsite Brise du Lac at Cabanac, a few km downstream of St Geniez, provides a good base for anglers who wish to night fish in this area. There is a freezer for bait and boats for hire at 10 euros per 24 hours. There are caravans to hire and an 8 person flat for rent.

Night fishing on right bank from 200m downstream of Pont de Lous to EDF dam wall. Regulations require casting less than 100m at night and the use of black leads. **Permits** for night fishing: Maurice Vayllet, *Cabanac, 12130 St Eulalie d'Olt* – tel, 1665474476 or at campsite – tel, 1665704070.

Lac de Croux (100ha): tr, p/b, pi, za, pe, ca, te, 100m wide, set in a beautiful broad green valley with wooded hills looking on. The lake is circum-navigated by a tourist road which makes access to the shoreline easier. Banks are sandy and of shallow incline, good spot is at Lincou half way west shore up by the bridge. Upstream of the plant on the left bank is also worth fishing. This water has a good reputation for its pike and zander: the main tributary is the Javret.

Barrage de Golinhac (57ha): located at Estaing, Lot basin downstream of Lac de Castelnau-Lassouts, tr, pi, p/b, za, pe, ca, te, few anglers fish here. Holds a good population of big carp. The water level is more consistent in summer. Upstream the banks become steep by Estaing and downstream towards the dam, so fish in the middle. From Estaing to the dam a boat is recommended. The reservoir was drained in 1992, carp average 8/10kg or more. Sweetcorn, tiger nuts, caovete nuts and crayfish flavour boiles all work well.

Directions: 10km downstream of Espalion access to right bank is by car parks at edge of RD920 by bar-restaurant Paradou, this spot is good for zander by the large retaining wall. Try on left bank by *plage des Peuplieres*, and by river Luzane outlet. Go via a dirt track for 3km on the left bank, turn off is just before *Pont d'Estaing*, follow through fields and stop at shore before Roquette farm and Luzanne feeder stream. The water turns red after rain. The remainder of the lake is best fished by boat.

Lac de Gourde (16ha): tr, p/b, pi. Access by dirt track is ok, from the campsite at lac de Pareloup drive north for a few km. This is a nice lake in a lovely setting with lots of wildfowl. Fishing restricted to the lower zone where there are large pike. It is especially good towards the dam. Trout reach at least 1kg, boats are banned.

Barrage de Maury-Aveyron (167ha): aka lac de La Selves or, lac de Saint-Amans-des-Lots, tr, p/b, pi, pe, ca, te. This is a big, lovely water. V-shaped in plan. Split at its apex, the fast flowing feeder rivers, Selvet (north arm) and Selves (west arm) define its two main arms. ¾ of shoreline is steep. **Directions**: However better access provides good fishing sport by following road from the dam (west shore) along Selvet arm of reservoir via Saint-Amans de Cots highway in a north east direction towards Touluch (west shore).

Try in the vicinty of, river Selvet where it enters the lake (top of reservoir). This is due to fish expectation of good food supply and the invigorating current. The shore here is shallow and sandy, there is a campsite and water sports centre nearby. Next, the road follows south towards arm of Selves where the more important fishing occurs. Arrive at d'Oustrac peninsula where there is a shallow bank, making good place to fish and launch boat from. Where the river Selves enters the lake (south east shore) there is an excellent fishing spot adjacent to the car park. Finally by crossing the road bridge, locate the campsite at Romiquiere next to which is a wide shoreline.

Barrage de Villefranche de Panet (192ha): the road goes right around the whole lake making it by far the easiest place to fish in the area, tr, p/b, pi, za, pe, ca, te. Dominated by the famous tower of Peyrebrune (never heard of it!), this splendid lake at Villefranche de Panet is set in shallow wooded basin. There is a nice footpath to take over the dam wall by the town. 44k mlong, 500m wide, all water sports are catered for. The banks are shallow: it stays shallow for quite a way out into the lake.

It is full of fish and easy to find a spot away from the noise. A good spot is upstream of the dam (bottom of lake) towards where the l'Arrance feeder stream enters the lake (top of lake). Fish here expect food to come down the current in the fast water (flow created by turbines). French anglers fish *l'Anglais* style here due to the longer casting distances required. Try catching trout on worms in l'Arrance stream.

Barrage de Pareloup (1240ha): also known as lac de Salles-Curan holds 170million cubic feet of water (note the French retain imperial), 40m deep, 120km of shoreline. Biggest lake in the region and 5th largest in France. Access via bank-side paths is very good, boat fishing is permitted (as are power boats!). Boat hire available. Loads of different swims; from rocky outcrops to sandy beaches and big islands.

Lac Pareloup forms part of a 5 lake system spread over an area of 1,800ha on *the plateau vallone du Cevezou* between Grand Causses and Segala. The other 4 lakes are *Lac Gourde* (1st cat.), *lac Bages* (1st cat.), *Pont de Salors* and Villefranche-de-Panet are 2nd cat. public, boats allowed.

Had a reputation as a, big hard carp water prior to its latest draining. Not many fish but it has potential. Mobile carp shoals are easily spotted in the clear water. Seek protection from the prevailing westerly wind in a multitude of arms and inlets. As fishing can be slow, choose your swim carefully.

Pareloup is known to anglers as the "kingdom of pike and zander". Zander grow to 4/5kg and sometimes as much as 8kg, especially in June.

But paradoxically during the summer this type of sport can slow down. The best spot to catch them is on retenue de Pareloup in the area where the old submerged river channel bed was flooded. Here is also a good place to catch carp: because of the very large crayfish that they feed upon, they grow big. Hundreds of pike are caught every year to over 1m in length, especially at beginning of winter in the many lake bays. But the pike fishing is not exceptional for the area. Another good spot for pike and zander is the barrage de Pinet at Saint Rome.

The **campsite** at *Camping du Soleil* has parking, bar and battery charging for boat trolling motors. Boat hire is located around the lake-shore.

Night fishing is permitted at l'eau des Vernhes from 30th September to 1st June. Camping at Caussanal on north arm, left of bridge. There is a speed limit for boats in this zone, so it offers peaceful times. Pareloups banks are less inclined than at Pont de Salors and the campsites are more pleasant ie less commercial.

Directions: 40km from Rodez and Millau: from Rodez take *RN88* up to Primaube then *RN911* and *D993*, 2.5km after Pont de Salars up to Salles-Curan. Then *D577* and *D176*, now make turn for lake.

Barrage de Pont de Salors (190ha): tr, pi, pe, ca, te, dam is situated just a few hundred metres up from Salors near Rodez. The lake is 6km long, 150-200m wide. Very big carp present. In spite of its tight meandering course it is a popular place for water sports. There are boat clubs, public spaces and campsites by the shore plus 10km of quiet easy access shoreline away from the swimming areas and boats, exclusively for the fishermen.

Directions: a) Left arm of lake, the banks are a bit steep but access is ok. Fish at end of left arm via Mejanes road, where La Cadouse stream enters the lake (eastern end). Try also at *Pont de Mejanes*, Merican road and d'Auzuech road; where there is a big fishing area on the left bank. b) Right arm. Upstream of Montredon peninsula, fish at top end of lake under the *Pont de Moulin-Fabre* (north east shore). The water gets deep very quickly in places so you don't have to cast far to reach the big'uns. The zone of *Moulin-Fabre* is particularly good at spawning time when thousands of carp gather by La Viaur feeder stream. Recently pike and zander catches have improved greatly.

Barrage de Sarrans: at Saint-Geneviere-sur-Argence, on river Truyere a tributary of the Lot, (trout, pike, zander, carp, tench) 2km long, average width 300m, 100m deep at dam wall which is 133m tall. Set in a beautiful location with steep wooded banks, the best access *a pied* is at *Presquile Laussac* where there is a boat launch and beach area. To the right is a sandy bottom and aquatic vegetation. The left arm has access above the bridge. The *Pont de Treboul* crosses the longest arm where the river Truyere enters the reservoir. Very deep with few anglers. Pike and zander rule the roost. There are very beautiful wild carp. **Directions**: 1 hour 30 minutes drive from Rodez. **Night fishing** is permitted.

Lac de Bannac (15ha): aka lac de Castelnau de Mandailles and lac de Cabenac. Located around towns of Martiel and Laramiere east of Villefranche, pi, za, bb. It is set in a pretty vale with shallow sloping shoreline. Access is good. The lake is divided in two. There is provision for 4km of bank for coarse fishing and 3km of bank for fly. Fish for the black bass with a fly, just tie a couple of fly droppers off your main line and attach a bubble on the end for casting distance. This technique really works well and is a lot of fun, especially when the bass strikes. Use poppers, streamers and insect replicas. At sheltered inlets cast from the bank to the bass holding up under the trees. Day tickets cost 3 euros. This is a family lake, it has a **campsite**, drinks kiosk, miniature golf, swimming pool. However, the swims are quiet and secluded.

Directions: from Villefranche de Rouerge take the D911 west and turn off south after Martiel for the lake. For local info: *AAPPMA, 8 quai del'hopital, 12200 Villefranche de Rouerge* te/fax, 0565451839.

Lac de Pinet (117ha): tr, p/b, pi, za, pe, ca, te, ba. **night fishing** at Le Masnaug, from Pont de Saint-Rome-de-Tarn to Pinct; **disabled access** at the dam and at dam by St. Rome de Tarn. The swims at the boat club on the beach have the best access, fishing by boat is really good

1st dam in a series of four EDF dams on the river Tarn. 7km long, 80 – 200m wide, located near the super Balsan falls at St Rome-de-Tarn. Access to both banks here is ok despite the vegetation. The relief changes completely from the *embouchure* to the *Abandon* brook, 8km further on. Here the water is sandwiched between two hills of rock. The banks are inaccessible here except by means of narrow steep paths. This is certainly an imposing and beautiful landscape that can be observed best by crossing via sealed roads on the right bank where you approach the lake 500m before the small arm of *l'Abandon*, next to the village of Pinet. All water sports are banned up to 1km from the dam.

Lac de Panzet: small water, well known specimen venue, many big fish stocked illegally from adjacent river Lot. However crime doesn't pay as these carp have now been stolen again to stock private commercial lakes in the region. This process has been so efficient that there are no big fish left.

The **River Lot** has a strong current around Pont de Port d'Agres area because of the activities from numerous nearby *barrages* e.g. Estaing and Sarrans therefore it is usual to employ heavy weights of 180 grammes minimum weight. In order to hold bait to the bottom. In addition expect to position rods at a 45 degree angle. Water is released constantly except during July and August when the river level is kept low for holiday makers' water sports.

At La Chaussee de Flagnac the river Lot channel is 4m deep, with deeper holes reaching 7/8m in depth, the channel is roughly 80-100m in width. Carp seek out sunken timber so be prepared to tie strong kevlar leaders. Baits to recommend include chick peas, tiger nuts and a favourite, fruity/flesh coloured boiles. Mirror carp make up 80% of the carp population. 700m downstream it is 1.5m deep, the same width so use the same tactics and baits.

The river Lot offers, **night fishing** from Chaussee de Floirac to Chaussee de Roguelonge. The first night fishing zone, at Capdenac offers a few interesting features e.g. a small blind arm, a water outlet, a good river bend and an old sluice. Many swims are best accessed from boat, which can be launched opposite the snack bar. **Disabled access** provided. At the second zone at Clayrou, fish only in designated zones. Much of bank here is private, so ask around. In particular: a) from Pont de *Port d'Agres* to the Roquelongue highway. b) Floirac highway (Cuzac/Asprieres): to Frontenac highway.

Fishing the **River Lot at Capdenac: directions**: from RN140 for 7km, at Capdenac go in direction of Decazeville, Rodez. Principal access is on right bank bordering the main road at Clayrou opposite the mobile snack bar. This river stretch includes many good swims including a small arm, two bends and an old lock. It is possible to fish the left bank by travelling via Capdenac towards Asprices for 4km then take left for Venet and continue up to river channel. There are places for boat launching.

The next stretch is from Moulin d'Assier up to the road at Capdenac. Access to the right bank is good between the two bridges. Left bank access is at bois de Las Farques. A concrete embankment can be fished from near the road bridge on the left bank.

The next brief stretch is by the municipal campsite where the bank is kept in good order. The exit to this stretch is marked by an ancient sewer outlet on the left bank and opposite by a water extraction plant, both features have good access. Close by is an old gravel pit still connected to the main channel where the fish have made a home.

A long road follows and the right bank is accessible up to the tunnel at Livinhac le Bas. The channel flows straight for 1km and is 2.5m deep with a gravel bottom. Further along access is next possible from Soulie along. This water is popular here with pike and zander specialists from the boat. Perch fishing is good here to boot.

The left bank is accessed at Vitrac via farm tracks. Launch your boat above the power station or why not try fishing by the *embouchure de Guirandol* opposite the island.

Next stretch, access points are rare. There is a splendid sealed bank 100m after *Pont de Madeline*. And on right bank by the riding school. In spite of apperances this section is public. Upstream the depth is 2m with much aquatic vegetation.

Travel up the same road (*D86*) to next section where the bank space is softly inclined and a good boat launch spot is by the mini bamboo plantation. The river coarse goes towards Carjac and Cahors. Next place is at a paved section upstream from *Pont de Toirac*, from here it is very pretty. Right bank only for **night fishing**. However night fishing is possible elsewhere on private land if you ask kindly.

Permits: At Capdenac by *bureau tabac* opposite the *Hotel de Ville*. Or at *articles de pêche* in the high street. Also try at the municipal campsite by the banks of the river Lot. This is an ideal family spot where you can **night fish** while the kiddies are sleeping.

Good eating can be found at *l'auberge de la Diege* 1km from the centre of Saint Julien d'Empare. A *hypermarché* is near Fignac. Near Pont de Madeline is a riverside restaurant *Bellerive* and one other La Madelon specializes in meat dishes. 2km downstream *Le Murier de Viels* restaurant sports a great menu.

CHARENTE-MARITIME (17)

Regional angling advice:	(AAPPMA) Club Carpe de la Gaule Niortaise Fédération de Deux Sevres pour la Pêche 33 rue du Galuchet 7900 Niorot tel 0549092333 fax, 0549732417 email: peche79@club-internet.fr
General information:	Tourisme and Pêche: Charente-Maritime Villa Musso (1st floor) 62 Cours National – BP 142 17115 Saintes – Cedex tel, 0546950717 fax, 0546976817 email: tourisme.et.peche.17@wanadoo.fr
Permits:	Pacific Pêche Zone Mendes France, Niort Tel, 0549336434 La Piouille Bar Tabac Presse – Arcois Tel, 0549353706

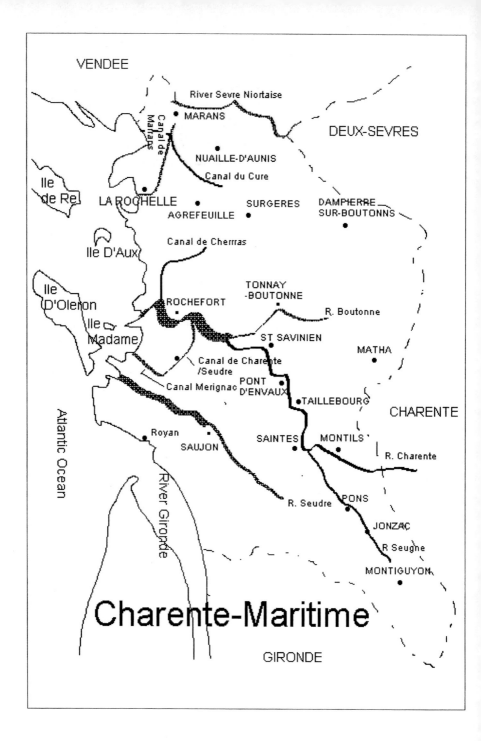

Licenses and regulations: *Carte Vacances* cost 31 euros and are valid from 1st June to 30th September and are valid for all rivers, lakes and night fishing. 4 rod limit. *Carte Journaliere;* costs 9 euros is valid from 1st June to the end of the year, on 2nd cat waters. *Carte jeune* for under 16's costs 22 euros.

Pike and zander season runs from 3rd Saturday in April to last Sunday in January. Trout season runs from 2nd Saturday in March to 3rd Sunday in September.

The main river systems are all 2nd catagorie public. River Sèvre Nortaise flows 150km west into the Atlantic above La Rochelle. River Mignon. Le Canal Marans-La Rochelle flows from La Rochelle north to Marans. Le Canal de Charras. Le canal Charente-Seudre flows From Marennes up to Tonnay Charente. River Charente flows up to Rochhefort from below Saintes further south. River Boutonne is fishable downstream of (RN 150 Pt du Faubourg Taillebourg near St Jean d'Angely) to its *embouchure* further west with the River Charente.

Disabled access at: Canal Charente-Seud re (l'ecluse de Beaugeay), Lieu Bellevue (2 pontoons), at Pilley Montherault. Canal de Charras-Saint Laurent de la Pree, after *l'ecluses*; after *Pont d'Ardilleres*. Canal de Marans-La-Rochelle-Rompsay Sevre- Niortaise at Marans (Riviere du Moulin des Marais). River Tonnay-Boutonne: at Boutonne Camping, upstream of bridge, left bank; and at St-Jean d'Angely: *quai de Bernouet*.

Monsieur Francois Xavier Secher from the *Tourisme & Pêche Office* in the Charente-Maritime department is an expert on fishing the River Charente, he kindly takes time to share his expert knowledge with us.

"This is the best carp river in the department. The carp are numerous, of fighting spirit and infrequently fished. Mostly commons or mirrors, their elongated forms are typical of river, as opposed to the fatter lake fish.

9kg specimens are par for the course, although 13kg to 18kg fish are well represented. Fish of a record 22.6kg have also been spotted. The actual record for the river Charente is 22.6kg but even bigger carp exist!

The Charente is relatively slow moving current; most of the time the Charente is an easy fish. This river is also especially rich in larger quality

---

fish.

Select your swim by observing the areas where the carp break the surface, obstacles in the water (such as bridge supports or trees) and look for the holes in the riverbed.

The Charente is rich in natural food sources, however, the ground bait here is efficient and useful, especially when used in quantity as the bigger bream (up to 5 lbs) consume a small quantity of the bait and the current disperses the rest. 6 lbs of grain and 4 lbs of boilies daily are necessary during the best part of the year - from March until May and from August until October. The standard fishing tackle is sufficient - a rod which resists a weight of 3.5 lbs, a weight of 90 - 110 gms, an ensemble anti-tangle on a line of 0.30 mm and a hair-rig.

Attention. The Charente is a river that flows into the sea and is, as a result, subject to the tides. The tides, which have a coefficient of more than 70° change the sense of flow, reversing the current for several hours and at times disturbing the fishing. The influence of the tide is felt, as far as *La Baine* in the village of Chaniers, 8 kilometres upstream of Saintes. The touches are frequent when the current is normal or non-existent, however, as soon as the current re-turns the touches stop. In this case place the hook bait upstream of the ground bait.

The tide depends on the Moon, which also influences the behaviour of the carp. It is for this reason that the bites during the 1st quarter of the new moon will pull you out of the deepest sleep! The fishing is much more productive in the evening or in the morning although when the weather is over-cast or cloudy touches are frequently felt during the daytime.

The fishing stretches. Taillebourg, Bussac/Charente, Courbiac, the Centre of Saintes, and Dompierre/Charente. The Courbiac stretch is one of the best sectors of the department and also has the advantage of being easily accessed, even by vehicle. Accessed only on one side (see directions in the *topo-guide Parcours de pêche en Saintonge*) as the railway runs parallel on the other side, this stretch hides big quantities of Carp.

Night-fishing. There are 27 well-defined stretches (marked by signposts) which permit Carp fishing at night (all year round). The three listed below are the most interesting in the immediate area of Saintes.

Courbiac: On the left bank, from, the point where the white track-road reaches the river: and in the sense of the white track-road, until the track-road leaves the Charente's riverbank, (opposite the Chateau of Bussac on the opposing riverbank). This stretch is approximately 1200 metres long.

Saintes town Centre: From the *Pont Palissy* at the bottom of the high street as far as the point where the canal and the Charente split up: uniquely on the side of the Arc de Triomphe! This **night zone** then continues approximately 500 m upstream on the Charente, (still on the right bank), and finishes at the tributary ditch.

Courcoury: From the Bac at Chaniers on the left bank to 500 metres upstream of the Bac.

River Seugne. This tributary of the Charente offers a very different Carp-fishing stretch. La Seugne is a small river about 20 metres wide, bordered by healthy green vegetation, where it is possible to take Carp of 9kg or more in the numerous dips which punctuate the course of this river. The more interesting swims start at Colombiers, which is accessed by taking the RN 137 direction Bordeaux-Pons. The bridge on the road to the Lijardière, situated nearer to Pons is an excellent carp-fishing area. The holes in the riverbed are sometimes as deep as 5 metres and are often circular.

River weeds are often found in this area as well as fallen branches and submerged tree-trunks and the clarity of the water leads to suspicious carp. However, ground baiting in advance using sweet corn allows you to take carp of 13.6kg, although the average size catches are around 6-8kg. Line breakages are frequent as the carp of La Seugne are cunning and powerful. In order to further discover these fishing stretches the association "Tourism and fishing in Charente Maritime" propose a specially edited guide for fishermen, entitled "fishing Stretches in Saintonge". To obtain a translation of this guide at the reasonable price of 20 FF, you're welcome to write to Monsieur Sécher at the address below or pass directly at *Tourisme et Pêche* offices, on the 1st floor of the Tourist Office/Office de Tourisme at Saintes.

Saujon. L'Etang de la Lande: This lake of around 4 hectares is sprinkled with little islands and is very partitioned. The disadvantage of this pond is that, being recently constructed, shade is very lacking. To access this lake, take the RN 150 in the direction of Royan. On arrival at Saujon, take the 2nd exit on your right, signed Rochefort, Le Gua. At the top of slope, turn left at the "STOP", direction Le Gua, then left again green sign posted *Le Lac* and finally left again before the first house.

This is an interesting area of water to fish using *l'Anglais*, wagglers, swing tip or quiver tip rigs and the record here is a carp of 18.1kg. Common Carp and Mirror Carp of 7 to 9kg are common. In order to attain more bites it is better to fish nearer to the islands. This is a free to fish lake provided you have the *Carte de Pêche*."

River Sèvre Niortaise: *secteurs de peche*: 77.9 km of fishing bank in total. Fish all along the river. **Night fishing** at St Jean de Liversay, lot no 49, a 2700 stretch on the right bank. And Lot 19, a 1664m stretch on the left bank. Also at Marans, Lot no 52 in part; the *barrage de tête* (beginning lot no 22) up to confluence with the river Moulins (lot no 51) on both banks.

The text may appear complicated but just remember that you can fish in all areas except the no-fishing reserves, these are well sign posted. The no-fishing reserves are found around *écluses* and *barrages* (50m either side) along the river channel.The *lots* (e.g. *PK123*) are sequenced in a downstream numerical order; starting inland (small values) from east to west, towards the Atlantic coast (largest numbers).

More Night fishing in Charente-Maritime

River Moulin des Marais: at Marans, 200m upstream of bridge on the two rivers. From the bridge to the confluence of the diversion DDE on the right bank.

River Curé: at d'Andilly, from *Pont de Réhon* to *Pont de Sérigny* (RN 137) for a 2300m stretch of right bank.

Canal de Marans à La Rochelle: at d'Andilly, Lot no 7, a 2350m stretch from *Pont d'Andilly* to to Siphon des Bois on the right bank. And at Villedoux/d'Andilly, Lot no 8 from *Pont du Prieur* to *l'écluse* *d'Andilly* for a 2100m stretch of right bank. Also at Ciré d'Aunis, from *Pont de Lagord* up to 500m upstream of the two rivers. Finally at d'Ardillieres, from *Pont d'Ardillières* to *barrage de Portfache*, on a 600m stretch oof the two rivers.

River Boutonne: at Tonnay-Boutonne, 800m stretch upstream of *Pont de Tonnay* on the left bank. and at Cabariot fromiron bridge up to the *reserve du barrage de Carillon* on the right bank.

Canal de Brouage: at Beaugeay, from the Beaugeay highway for 500m upstream towards the Canal Charente-Seude, right bank.

Canal de Charente-Seudre: at Hiers-Brouage, from the Mérignac revolving bridge to *La Buse Noir*, 1200m of right bank.

Canal de Charras: at Cire-d'Aunis: night fishing zone on both banks 500m upstream of *Pont de Lagord*. And at: Ardilleres on both banks from bridgee to *Barrage de Portefache*.

River Seugne: at *Pons, R. Diet* sports field, by the two ditches, 200m stretch.

River Cher: at Preuilly/St Thorette, Bourges, night fishing zone lot B19 from *CD113* to the bridge.

River Charente: night fishing at weekends only:
a) Le Mung, from the water supply point of *UNIMA* water intake to 500m downstream on the left bank.
b) At Saintes (Courbiac), from the white road to opposite the *Chateau de Bussac/Charente*, a 1200m stretch of left bank.
c) Also at Saintes, Lots no 9-10-11, from *Pont Palissy* to irrigation canal no 1 at the Pallue meadow, 1500m of right bank.
d) At Courcoury, upstream of Chaniers ferry, 500m of left bank.
e) At Rouffiac and Dompierre/Charente, from *ruisseau le Pérat* to Dompierre/Charente ferry, 5000m of left bank.
f) At Dompierre/Charente, from the ferry up to place known as *Sainte Marie*, 1500m of right bank.
g) At Les Gonds, from *Bras de gate Bourse* towards Rousson, 2000m of left bank.

The River Charente – a closer look

"Saintes on the River Charente, is situated 20 minutes from the Atlantic coast, between La Rochelle and Bordeaux, is better known for it's Roman ruins Saintes.

The average weight of local takes can be announced at 10 kilos, with a majority of the carp between 8 and 12 kilos. However, a high density of carp between 12 and 20 kilos can be seen with an Echo sounder.

The best swims are spread 15 km each side of Saintes Knowing the habits if not the psychology of the carp, here are some of the methods and tips used by the french carpistes (who're incidentally, a dedicated breed of fishermen!). The following summary is designed to give a helping hand and an insight into the habits and behaviour of the French carp.

The choice locals bait takes into account the season. During the springtime the carp become active from around the beginning of April. As a result, it's best to favour boilies rich in carbohydrates and grain, (proportioned 2/3 and 1/3). As for the quantity necessary, this varies between 3 and 5 kilos depending of the temperature. From the beginning of June, the use of smaller grains as well as little boilies is a good way to deceive the carp which are usually more occupied by their reproduction than their stomach. Towards the end of July, at the end of the reproductive period, the carp are more influenced by the temperature and the oxygen content of the water. The dosage of the bait should be adapted accordingly as during the hotter periods, the carp are more interested in finding oxygen rather than boilies and thus the dosage can be reduced. In spite of all these difficulties, the fishing can be very fruitful if a few easily digestible boilies are spread over the feeding zones.

The real action starts from around the 15th of August. The first drop in temperature sees the activity of the carp increase rapidly. Don't hesitate to bait in large quantities, (e.g. 10 kilos of which 7 of grain, 3 of boilies). The consummation varies between 50 and 100 boilies per day.

As far as the composition of the boilies and their flavourings are concerned, I have found the flavouring to be less important than the actual composition. The warmer the water, the less protein needed in the boilies. During the summer, boilies rich in carbohydrates should be favoured and the flavourings sugary or fruity such as strawberry, or fruit cocktail which seem to work most efficiently.

During the winter, my choice goes to the spiced flavourings associated with essential oils and used in conjunction with a mix rich in bird food, and high in protein, (over 60 %). Boilies with a base of casein, lactalbumine and powdered milk also give recognisable results used with flavourings such as chocolate malt, butterscotch, maple cream or milk cream, especially in springtime. The flavouring most appreciated remains the scopex mixed at 30 % to 50 % with the coconut flavouring and with a protein content of only 50 %. No matter what season, boilies with a base of propylene glycol or ethyl alcohol can be used, knowing that this combination always gives good results.

As for rigs, I find that a hair-rig gives excellent results, above all when used in conjunction with a bolt-rig. The weight of the leads used varies between 90 and 150 grams depending on the current and the distance fished. The presence of an anti-tangle tube can turn out to be more than useful in order to protect the mainline in swims where the obstructions are of important size. A shock-leader of plaited Kevlar is also indispensable from time to time.

The hook line, we tend to keep at 25 cm the majority of the time, although during the reproductive period a hook line of around 80cm will allow you takes in spite of the reticence of the carp.

It is worth knowing that the carp of the River Charente are little educated and even the simplest rigs turn out to be more than efficient. Taking your time to choose your swim, taking into account obstacles, etc. is of capital importance, as noting their natural feeding zones and preferred environments greatly increases your chances of not just taking carp but also of beating that ever present and ever-so-tempting record. ("English Angler beats french record!"). 3 night fishing zones are also available (from the bank and vegetal baits only).

I hope you do enjoy the challenge and fighting spirit of the French carp. Good Luck – Francois Xavier.

Night fishing is permitted on the following *plan d'eaus*: at La Rochelle: **plan d'eau Villeneuve Les Salines, Lac no1**. And at Saujon: **plan d'eau La Lande**.

And at other waters in Deux-Sevres region: a) **Plan d'eau Monniere et Fourmond,** next to river Sevre Nantaise at Moncoutant. c) **Plan d'eau Pierre Beaufort,** river Thovet, Parthenay. d) 410m of left bank, river Sevre Niortaise, 50m downstream of Fenouille and Epron mill roads, at St Martin de St Maixent in the *appt. de fedration Etrees* and *Creche*. e) Right bank of river Thovet at Thouars (375m stretch of bank). f) Right bank of river Thovet by La Chase at Thovars (360m stretch). g) **Plan d'eau la Chaiz**, river Ton at Bressuire. h) **Plan d'eau de St Jean de Angelys** (2ha), small lake that holds big carp to 25kg. However due to heavy stocking of smaller specimens you have to work hard to get to them. There are lots of 5-8kg fish. Night fishing on 300m stretch of bank. **Directions**: leave A10 by exit34.

Plan d'eau Nuaille-d'Aunis: night fishing permitted. **Les etangs de Minas**; camping nearby, one carp lake, one zander and pike lake. **Plan d'eau Heurtebise**: at Jonzac, night fishing permitted by river Overe at d'Argenton-Chateau. **Plan d'eau de Baron d'Esqueyroux**: at Montendre: night fishing permitted. Plan d'eau de Boutonne: **night fishing** from Tonnay to Cabriot. And on adjacent river Boutonne, from *Pont du Faubourg (D 18)* to the footbridge on the two rivers.

VENDEE (85)

Regional angling advice: Email: federation.peche.vendee@ wanadoo.fr

Fédération de la Vendee de Pêche
10 bis, rue Haxo – BP673 – 85016
La Roche-sur-Yun, Cedex
Tel, 0251371905, fax, 0251653413

École de Pêche:

Maurice Bussignes at, les Sables d'Olonne
tel, 0663100924 (m).

Les Lucs sur Boulogne
Gilles raynard
tel, 0251312336, 0616402769 (m)

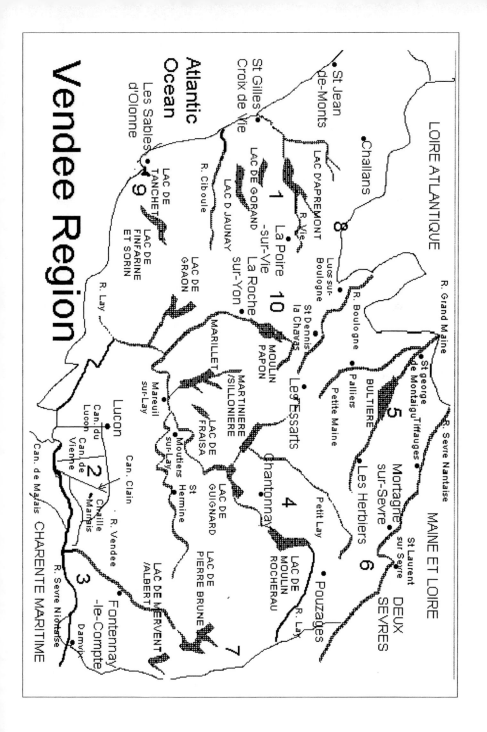

4,500km of waterways, 1,300ha of lakes. The *département Vendee* is bordered in the north by the river Sèvre Nantaise; it is 125km in length and flows into the river Loire at Nantes. And in the south by the river Sèvre Niortaise and Le Marais wetlands. Night fishing for 20 sections on *plan d'eaus*. Carp, 3-10kg are a common sight, 15kg is tops.

When visiting this area, look out for the sign **Vacances Pêche en Vendee.** It denotes accommodation that caters specially for anglers. It covers the whole range, from *gites*, hotels and campsites. To qualify as fishing lodges they have to be situated less than 1km from the bank side. For more information, go to: www.vendee-tourisme.com

Regulations and Licenses: *Carte Journaliere* – 8 euros, permitted to night fish on lakes and rivers. Under 12's go free, obtain a *Carte Verte Gratuite. Carte Vacances* – 30 euros, permits night fishing included. Pike and zander season, 18/4 - 27/1. A night light with 10watt minimum power is compulsory when night fishing.

Disabled access

a. La Sèvre Nantaise, at Pommeraie, Epesses, St Laurent-sur-Sevre (3 pontoons), Mortagne-sur-Sèvre, St Aubin des Ormeaux, Tiffauges and Cugand.
b. River Crume: (tributary of Sevres Nantaise) *Le Pre du Bateau* near Tiffauges.
c. La Maine at: St Hilaire se Loulay.
d. Le Petit Maine: Chavagnes in Pailliers.
e. La Boulogne: St Philbert de Bouaine.
f. Le Lat: St Pexine, Moutiers-sur-Lay, Mareuil and Peault.
g. Lac de Retenue de Borrage d'Apremont, at Mouche.
h. Étang des Ouches du Jaunay, at Martinet
i. Le Jaunay at:Aiguillon-sur-Vie
j. Canal l'eglise at: Chaille les Marais
k. Lac de Retenue de Barrage de l'Angle Guinard, at Chantonnay.
l. River Vendee at Gué de Velluire, after the café le Guétreén.
m. Lac de Coex: at La Chaize-Giraud (zone de loisirs), park by Filatoire (mill).
n. River l'Yon: after pont de Chaille.

o. Barrage de l'Angle Guignard: at start of Moulin Neuf and Touchegray.

Lac du Marillet and Moinie: after *petanque* area, towards sports centre at Mareuil, after pont de Lavaud at Peault.

The following angling locations are represented on the *département* map in numerical order.

1. Halfway up the Vendee coastline, around **St Gilles-Croix-deVie**, and inland. **Permits**: local *bar-tabacs* in each town or tackle shops. And at: *Camping Le Pin Parasol, Lac du Jaunay.*

- a) **Lac du Gué Gorannd** (30ha): at St Reverend, bb. Also try the adjoining river Gue Gorand: on both banks at Coex, St Reverend and Aiguillon.
- b) **River Jaunay**: at Aiguillon sr Vie, on right bank as you leave la Roche Blanchet up to C.D. no38 at Givrand.
- c) **Zone de Marais de Breme**: a number of canals.
- d) **Lac de Barrage de Jaunay** (114ha): ca, p/b, za, pi. Long narrow water, 60-120m wide but 5km long. Carp average 5/7kg, 10kg+ is a rare catch. However a Dutch angler caught one to 21kg+. Camping close by. **Night fishing**, zone a) 1.3km stretch, from upstream of *Pont de la Baudriere* (left bank) to edge of Baudriere. Zone b) 1.5km stretch, downstream of *Pont de la Baudriere* (right bank) to *la Baie de Chateaulong.*
- e) **Étang des Ouches du Jaunay** (1.75ha): at Martinet, pe, ga, te, ca. Has good family facilities and **disabled access**.
- f) **River Ligneron**: fish from Notre-Dame de Riez (best spot) to *Pont Gue* towards Roux.
- g) **River Vie**: fish from *Pont Pas Opton* towards *Pont de la Musardiere.*

2. **South Vendee**: between *Marais desseche* and *Marais mouille.* **Permits**: *Café des Sports, 10 rue du 8 Mai, Chaille les Marais.* And at: *Articles de pêche, Masson, Mareuil sur Lay.* Also, at: *Boulangerie Morrilleau, Vix. École de Pêche*: *M. Augereau, 82, rue des Huttes – 85370 Nalliers –* tel, 0251309588/0684061042 Map

- a) This area has **120km of canals to fish**. Pi, za, pe, ee, p/b.

b) **Étangs des La Source and Baritaudieres**: just south of Le Langon.

Le Marais Poitevin and Marais Breton

This large re-claimed freshwater wetland nature reserve on the Atlantic coastline is an excellent big fish venue. Le Marais is the second largest wetland area in France after the Camargue. It is situated south of the Pays de Retz, 30km after Saint-Gilles.

Le Poitevin area has contrasting dry (*Les Marais Dessseche*) and wetland (*Marais Mouilles*) zones and is supplied by La Sèvre Niortaise, La Vendee and Le Lay. In the middle, *Le Marras Desseche* offers a barren open flat landscape only broken by the pattern of reed beds along the channels. Hydraulic sluice gates regulate the water levels. The fishing, here is excellent. Expect to catch eels, carp, pike and zander.

---

3. **Damvix**: south Vendee, *école de pêche* for tourists in July and August on Wednesday afternoons from 2.30 – 6pm, M. Damour tel, 0251871169. *Turisme* tel, 0251872301 at Niort. **Permits**: *Bar Le Mazeau, Damvix. Tabac-presse, rue du Faienciers, L'Ile d'Elle.*

   a) **River Sèvre Niortaise**: p/b, za, pi, ca, te, 1.5km stretch, right bank from Damvix to Niort. And upstream at L'Ile d'Elle.
   b) **La Sèvre Niortaise**: **night fishing** on a 1.5km stretch, left bank from confluence of the Sèvre Niortaise to *Pont du Bourg (D104),* and right bank 0.5km stretch from Damvix to Canal du Nouveau Béjou, at Damvix.
   c) 3km of **night fishing** in two zones, i. Lot 17, 1850m stretch, right bank of Canal du Sablon from PK 42.725 to PK 44.186, at Vix the channel is 70m wide. ii. 1500m stretch of Sèvre Niortaise, Lot 18, left bank from PK 42.725 to PK 44.186, at St Jean deLiversay.
   d) **Plan d'eau** of 7km on Sèvre Niortaise, which winds between départements of the Vendee and Charente Maritme, 70m wide and 4.5m deep at Vix. Some big fish here.
   e)

4. **Chantonnay**: central Vendee. *École de Pêche*, M. Perrotin – tel, 0251943595. **Permits**: Pecheur des 2 Lays, avenue Mg Batiot, Chantonnay. At all the lakes there are restaurants, camping, and *chambres d'Hotes*. **Tourisme** tel, 0251944651.

a) **Barrage de l'Angle Guignard** (55ha): pi, za, p/b.

b) **Barrage de Moulin Rochereau** (127ha): at Chantonnay, p/b, za, pi, ca, e, p/b. Carp to 15kg, average size is 4-8kg. **Night fishing** at Sigournais and Monsireigne on both banks of *Pont de la Louraie*, to *Pont de Bourdin.* Restaurant-bar, camping, sailing.

c) **Barrages de la Silloniere and Martiniere** (76ha): p/b, pi, za, ca.

d) **Lac du Marillet and Moinie** (124ha): at Chateau Guibert, p, z, c, p/b, bb, near Mareuil sur Lay. Good head of carp but most are small, *piosson chat* are pests, carp up to 10kg are considered quite a catch. **Night fishing** on a 4km stretch, from Moulin Martin to the dam.

5. **Chavagnes en Palliers**: north Vendee, **permits**: M. Clergeau, Hôtel-Bar de la place. And at: Ma Champagne, *jardinerie* (nursery), route de Cholet, Montaigu.

a) **Barrage de la Bultière** (72ha): at St Loup de Gast, ca, pi, pe, te, ga, a very new venue built in 1994, it was stocked immediately with carp from the nearby river Grande Maine and annually since from stock carp. The carp average 5kg occasionally up to 18kg. **Night fishing** on a 1.5km stretch, right bank from Les Roussieres to La Flatriere.

b) **River Maine**: za, pi, ca, ga, 65km stretch from Paillers up to Montaigu.

c) **Lac de la Chausseliere**: za, pi, ca, ga, **night fishing** on 0.5km stretch, on zone *réservée à la pêche*, at Gutonniere. For **permits** tel, 0240265391.

d) **Le lac des Vallées**: at Viellevigne, za, pi, ca, ga, **night fishing** on a 200m stretch, left bank of lake from a point located 50m downstream of *Pont de la Boussonière*, at Vieillevigne.

6. **Clisson**: north Vendee, **permits:** Tabac-journaux, 18, place de l'Eglise – 85610 Cugand. And at: Café des sports, Mouchamps.

a) **River Sèvre Nantaise**: ro, ch, va, pi, pe, si, ca, 30-40m wide, good spots at La Douciniere, Hucheloup, Gaumier and Fouques. A nice river to fish. Try downstream at St Aubin by bridge at Grenon, or further down at Mortagne-sur-Sevre, 6-20m wide, good spots at La Roche Bordon, Le Pre du Domaine and Le Grand Moulin.

Swims at Mallieuse and St Aubin des Ormeaux, river channel here is 15-30m wide and it increases to 100m in width at *Barrage St Aubin*. Deeper holes reach 4m in depth where the feeder streams run into the main channel and on bends. The local Aapma regularly stocks the river, common carp are the dominant species they are long muscular specimens reaching 5kg. Granite rocks in the channel will snap line. 16kg is the river carp record, caught at St Aubin. Locate best swims by traversing fields, why not make a turn for Rochard, near Montagne-sur-Sevre, between Evruness, downstream of Mortagne and St Aubin des Ormeaux. The fish here have never seen a boile before, sweetcorn is just as good. Cast to the carp by the water lilies. A new **night fishing** zone, downstream of Clisson.

b) **River Sèvre Nantaise**: **night fishing** on a 300m stretch, right bank upstream of Thovet to mill road at Mortagne Sur Sèvre. And on a 700m stretch of left bank of the old Rouet road, upstream, downstream to *l'embouchure* with river Crume, at Tiffauges.

c) **River Petit Lay:** 16km, stretch from *l'ecluse de Berton* at Le Boupere to Moulin Neuf at Ste Cecile, particulary good at Mouchamps where, there is a good footpath to the bank. **Camping** Le hameau du Petit Lay, by river bank.

d) **Étang de Haute Riviere**: directions: leave L'Oie by RN137 south towards St Vincent Sterlanges, very easy access and barbeque areas.

e) **Lac des Rivières** sur la Sevre Nantaise: at St Aubin des Ormeaux, **night fishing** on 1km stretch, zone 1. 500m of left bank from La Source, zone2. 500m of left bank from St Andre close to the barrage.

7. **Fontenay-le-Comte**: south Vendée. **Directions**: D938T, za, pi, pe, ca, p/b, for information on accommodation, ***tourisme*** tel, 0251008680 (Vouvant), **permits**: *Articles de Pêche, rue du port, Fontenay le Comte. École de pêche* - tel 0251690281 childrens lake at: *étang de la Vaudieu*.

a) **Barrage de Pierre Brune** (65ha): Vendée river basin, at Fontenay-le-Comte,

b) **Lac de Vouvant** (25ha): at Vouvant,

c) **Lac de Mervent** (128ha): p/b, za, pi, e. On leaving village of Mervent after the pont de la Vallee, find parking and boat ramp nearby. After the lake was drained in 1986 a tonne of Hungarian zander was stocked here, making this lake a paradise for the zander fisherman. **Night fishing** on a 1.6km stretch at Mervent, on both banks of the confluence of the *ruisseau des Verreries* to *pont de la Vallee* (D99).

d) **Lac de'Albert** (104ha): **directions**: D49, for St Michel le Cloucq, well stocked with carp averaging 4/6kg, some bigger up to 10/15kg going to 20kg ocassionally. New lake record is 25kg caught in December 2003. **Night fishing** on a 2.5km stretch, at St Michel le Cloucq and Foussais Payre. Both banks, from Marchandelle (left bank) and Ceppe a Picard road (right bank) to the dam.

e) **River Vendee**: 15km stretch from Fontenay downstream to Velluire, easy parking, barbeque area at Massigny (Chaix). **Night fishing:** a) lot no3, a 2.2km stretch b) left bank from Brillac upstream to national reserve of Messigny at Chaix.

f) **River Vendee**: **night fishing** on Lot no3 for a 2km stretch, left bank from Brillac to upstream at *reserve nationale de Massigny*, at Chaix. Signposted.

g) **River Lay**: pi, za, ca, te, br fish from Chantonnay to l'Aguillon-sur-Mer. Channel is 15-40m wide and 2/3m deep. Deeper holes reach 6m in depth: there are lots of trees making access often difficult.

Carp average 4/6kilos, but 10kg common carp are often landed, mirror carp reach 24kg, the *poisson chat* is a pest. On some stretches the carp seem to ignore boiles, sweetcorn is their prefered tucker, especially if you want big bags, but stick with boiles for the big'uns. Numerous locks constantly manage the channel's level. But this remains a good river for boat fishing. Broken lines often result due to submerged trees and branches.

Silures are caught at Moutiers-sur-Lay. Fish downstream and upstream of Mareuil-sur-Lay. And its tributary, the river L'Yon upstream to La-Roche-sur-Yon. There is no night fishing because the majority of banks are located on private property. **Permits**: *M. Poireaud (Flora Vert) Beugue l'abbe (Bar l'Escale), Lucon.*

8. **North central** Vendee, **permits**: *maison de la presse* SPS Negoce, *rue des Vignes gates – 85170 Les Lucs sur Boulogne.* And at: **Tourisme**, Place du Chateau, Apremont.

a) **River Boulogne**: ga, br, te, ca, pi, za, 30m wide, some nice stretches around Les Lucs-sur-Boulogne. And further downstream at Rocheserviere, fish from *Pont de l'Audronniere de Mormaison* past Rocheserviere up to Grimaudieres.

b) **Barrage de Apremont** (167ha): Nantes, p/b, pi, za, ca, bb, e. Carp to 15kg are a regular catch, some to 20kg+. Snags make it a tricky venue. **Night fishing** on 9km of bank, zone a) by Mache and Apremont, right bank of lake from water mill to a bridge situated 200m downstream of D50 pont de la Citadelle. Zone b) left bank, by Apremont and Aizenay downstream of *Pont de la Citadelle D50* to a point 250m upstream of dam wall. At Mache there is a swimming pool area, pedalos. At Apremont there is a beach with waterslide, pedalos, restaurants, barbeque area, sports area. At Aizenay there is a forest park and easy boat access.

9. **Les Sables d'Olonne**: on central Vendee coastline, **permits**: *Le Marlin Bleu, 20, quai Guine, Les Sables d'Olonne. Les Lacs de Poiroux:* south Vendee, around Talmont-St-Hilaire, **permits***: Café du phare, 21 avenue des Sables, Talmont St Hilaire.* **Ecôle de pêche** tel, 025151561886. **Permits**: *Mayor Sports, rue de Gaulle, Saint Gilles.* **Permits**: *Café, tabac La Madalon, Fenouiller.*

a) **Lac de Finfarine** (23ha) and Lac de Sorin (14ha): pi, za, pe, p/b, ga, br, ee, **night fishing** on a 400m stretch, left bank from river Davière, at Poiroux. ** **camping** with heated swimming pool, at Avrile, tel, 0251903597, same number for **n/f permits**. The lakes area has excellent tourist facilities.

b) **Lac de Tanchet** (6.5ha): a, nice family water at Les Sables d'Olonne, p/b, ga, te, pe, ee, the lake is seperated from the sea by a *digue* (sea wall). There are lots of carp present to 15kg. Surfers can prove a problem during the day. **Night fishing** on a 0.5km stretch right bank from l'hôtel Mercure to the overflow. **Directions**: D32B towards Talmont, between la Thalasso and the *beach des Presidents*, in front of the sea.

c) **Barrage des Vallees:** at Fenouiller, up to Pas Opton and various sections upstream of *Petit Pont.*

d) **River Jaunay**: at Givrand, **directions**: from St Gilles take the highway no38 south towards Givrand, at roundabout take a right, *la Rue des Bosses* in direction of the poplar trees to the river bank.

10. **La-Roche-sur-Yon**: central Vendee, for advice tel, 0251361323. These lakes have hosted several national angling championships (October 2000), in fact it is the home of ex world angling champion, Jean Pierre Lenezet who is famous throughout France. **Permits**: *Décathlon, centre commercial les Flanieres.*

   a) **Lac de Moulin Papon** (108ha): at Roche-sur-Yon, ca, te, ga, br, ee, pi, za, pe, aka Lac de la Roche-sur-Yon, 7km long, 6/7m deep in places, 10m deep at dam, holds a good head of carp, 6kg average size but going up to 15kg+, *silure* to 20kg+. **Night fishing** on left bank by l'Audouiniere, at Roche-sur-Yon. Boat club and sailing school. **Permits**: *La Pêcheur Yonnais* – tel, 51623085 they also provide information on neighbouring waters.
   b) **Lac de Graon** (68ha): at St-Vincent-sur-Graon, ca, te, ga, br, ee, pi, za, pe, **night fishing** on a 800m stretch, right bank from *Champ Hydreau.*

Lac de la Sillonière and La Martiniere (76ha):

SOMME (80)

900 km of rivers, 600ha of lakes, eels, pike, zander, carp, bream, tench, *poisson blanc*, sea trout and salmon. Public areas to fish include: river Somme, Canal de la Somme (excluding Canal de Raye-sur-Authie at Dourez and canal de la Maye or canal de Fazieres), Canal du Nord, sector of river Avre from *Pont de Moreuil*, upstream to confluence with the Somme, downstream; the lacs d'Heilly and Neuville-les-Loeuilly and all other lakes of 1st and 2nd catagorie. Catch salmon and sea trout at Lieu Dieu, on the river Bresles, this is classed as a 1st cat water.

All other information: Agence de l'Eau Artois-Picardie
200, rue Marceline - B.P. 818
59508 Douai Cedex
Tél.: 03 27 99 90 00
Fax: 03 27 99 90 15

River Somme Bassin

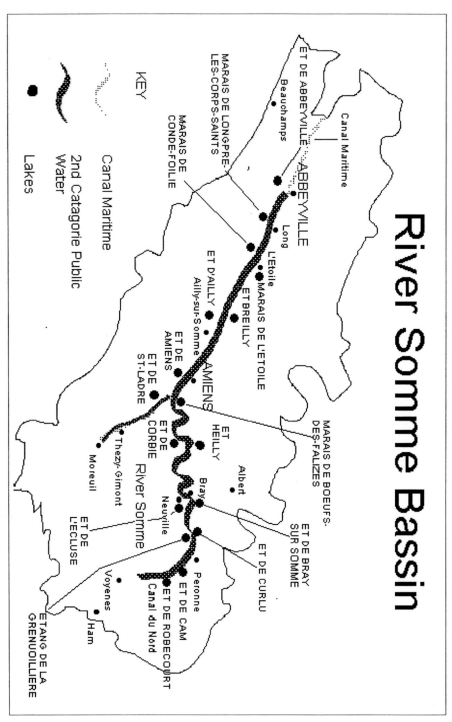

KEY

Canal Maritime

2nd Catagorie Public Water

Lakes

ET DE ABBEVILLE

MARAIS DE LONGPRE-LES-CORPS-SAINTS

MARAIS DE CONDE-FOLIE

Beauchamps

Canal Maritime

ABBEVILLE

Long

L'Etoile

MARAIS DE L'ETOILE

ET D'AILLY

ET BREILLY

Ailly-sur-Somme

ET DE AMIENS

ET DE ST-LADRE

AMIENS

ET DE CORBIE

ET HEILLY

MARAIS DE BOEUFS-DES-FALIZES

Albert

ET DE BRAY SUR SOMME

Thezy-Gimont

Moreuil

River Somme

Bray

Neuville

ET DE L'ECLUSE

ET DE CURLU

Peronne

ET DE CAM

ET DE ROBECOURT

Voyenes

Canal du Nord

Ham

ETANG DE LA GRENUOILLIERE

Regional angling advice:	Fédération de la Somme de Pêche (80)
	6, rue Reine Gambier
	BP 20 – 80450 Camon
	Tel, 0322702810 fax, 0322702811
	Email: Somme.FedePeche@wanadoo.fr
General information:	Tourisme: 21 rue Ernest Cauvin, - 80000 Amiens tel, 0322712269. www.somme-tourisme.com email: accueil@somme-tourisme.com

Regulations and Licenses: *Carte Jeune* (under 16's) – 13 euros. *Carte vacances* – 25 euros, valid from 1/6 – 30/9. *Carte Journaliere* – 7 euros. 1st cat waters open from 27th March to 3rd October. 2nd cat waters open all year. 4 rod limit on 2nd cat waters, 1 rod on 1st cat waters. Pike and zander season runs from 27th March to 3rd October on 1st cat waters. 17th April to 25th January on 2nd cat waters. Trout can be caught between 27th March and 3rd October.

Sea trout and salmon can be caught between 30th April and 31st October. Authorised zones include: La Somme from its estuary to the confluence with l'Avre (sea trout only), La Bresle, downstream of *Pont de la D25* at Sénarpont, and L'Authie, downstream of *Pont de la N25* at Doullens.

No use of groundbait or livebaits on all plan d'eaus and and canals. In addition, the use of maggots is prohibited on 1st cat waters.

Disabled access: Etangs Federation d'Heilly, *AAPPMA* Ailly-sur-Somme, AAPPMA de Long, Moreuil. Sites under construction (2003): at Bray, Boves, Conty, Thezy, Voyennes, Etangs Federaux de Neuville.

River Somme basin: there is excellent carp fishing: on 87km of 2nd cat public stretches of river Somme. Many public areas to fish on a lively sector of the river. From km marker 69.200 at Vaux-sur-Somme, to after Saint-Valery. Baits are restricted to vegetable based products e.g. no maggots or luncheon meat.

***Silure* hotspots**: on the river Somme at, Longpre, Ailly-sur-Somme, Saint Saveur, Amiens, Thézy-Glimont, and on canal de la Somme at, Bray, and river Ancre at Albert.

Permits: *Le Grand Bleu, St Valery, Abbeville* tel, 0322608246. *Bar des Voyageurs, Long* tel, 0322318712. *Café du Nord – 80890 Conde* – tel, 0322319174, *Hôtel La Bonne Cuisine, Conde-Folie, camping* – tel 0322319151. *Café de Sports, L'Etoile* – tel, 0322516798. *RDV des Pêcheurs, Gamanches* – tel, 0322261065, *Hôtel Le grand cerf du Lieu Dieu*, at Beauchamps.

Night fishing designates areas. From 2004 night fishing is permitted on the River Somme from PK69.200 at Vaux-sur-Somme to St Valery, an 87km stretch. There are many good carp to be caught in excess of 15kg.

Also, **night fishing** from junction with Canal du Nord and Canal de la Somme up to l'écluse d'Epenancout for a 1.9km stretch. More specifically, at Peronne: on public banks between the yatch club and the pont de Bazincourt. And from 105m downstream of *l'écluse d'Epancourt* up to *Pont de Briost*. Canal de La Somme: at Corbie, mirror carp to 21.75kg.

Département lakes

Étang AH11, Etang Denis Dubus, at Contoire-Hamel

Étang de St-Christ-Briost (47ha): mature, shallow water, covered in lilleys, common carp up to 9kg, mirror carp grow larger. 20 runs per night are not unusual. 5 swims available, you are rowed out to the swims by the owner. **Permits**: *Service Loisirs – Accueil Somme, 21, Rue Ernest-Cauvin, 8000 Amiens* – tel, 0322922639 fax, 0322927747.

Étang Malicorne and **La Ballastire**, at Abbcvillc. **Étang du Marais** aka en Bas du Wagon, Concours, Demi-lune, at Ailly-sur-Somme. **Étang des Prés d'Allaines**, at Allaines-Feuillancourt. **Étang de Dreuil**, at Dreuil-les-Amiens; 2 lakes: **Etang de Clara** at Glisy, section A211, at Glisy; **étang de La Ballastiere** at Argoeuves. **Étang du Marais**: at Boves. Near Ailley-sur-Somme aka d'en Bas Marais. Marais de Condé, *route d l'Etoile, lot A no238*, at Condé-Folie. **Étang no1, no2**, at Cony. **Etang no 3** at Roye.

Site de Neuville-les-Loeuilly – 2 lakes 3.5ha in total, plus 600m stretch of river Selle. Pegs for **disabled anglers** are coming on line (2004), provision of toilets, barbeque areas and more pontoons are on their way. These new lakes were opened in 2002, they are of modest size but there are lots of swims to choose from. **Étangs Breilly** and **d'Heilly** are gravel pits, 2.5 – 5m in depth, perch, tench, gardons and pike. The first lake is intended for specimen hunters. Marker bouoys exhibit the no-fishing area. The locals intend to move the *EDF* overhead power lines. **Directions**: located off route D8 after Cueilly driving north east.

L'étang Fédéral d'Heilly (15ha) 2 lakes, **disabled access**, toilet facilities, **night fishing**, public seating, spinning, for pike allowed during October, November and December.

Domaine des Iles-Offrey-Ham: 16ha of interconnected waters. **Étang Canard**, **Grand étang** (**night fishing** at Breilloire, lake near Flixecourt), **Étang Carron**. These lakes have an international reputation for excellent big carp fishing, commons to 27kg, several carp to 15kg in one session is not exceptional. 18 anglers at one time, so it's very exclusive. All swims are accessed by car, there is a bait freezer on site and toilets and showers. The baker visits the bank every morning at 9 o' clock, **reservations**: contact M. Caron – tel, 0323811055.

Domaine de la Valee: **Horshoe Lake** (52ha), formed from old blind arm of river Oise, it still retains a feeder stream to the main channel, this provides a good supply of natural food for the fish stock. 1.8km in length this is a very new and unspoilt private commercial fishery. It has good potential. Common carp up to 21.5kg, mirror carp reach 22.3kg (so far), toilets, showers and boat hire is on site.

Étang Sainte Marguerite and **Étang du Stade**: both at Gamaches, fish from *base nautique* to Moulin Araire lot no36. **Étang de Genonville**, at Moreuil. *Etang des commune et des groups*, at Long. **Étang des Dix**, at Longpre-les-Corps-Saints.

Plan d'eau de Ball-Trap-Saint-Saveur: **night fishing** on 5 zones, *Fer a Cheval, Base Nautique, Le Ranch, Le bourbier, La Rouiere*. **Étang communal**, at Prouzel. **Étang communal**, at Thezy-Glimont. **Étang de l'Aulnaie Gambart,** at Davenescourt; **Étang no3**, at Roye. **Étangs**, *lots* no331, at Loeuilly. **Étang Denis Dubus**, at Contoire-Hamel.

Étang du Moulin: at Frise-Peronne, quite shallow, lots of aquatic vegetation, good head of mirrors and commons to good size. 3 swims have easy access, one by boat, so only 4 anglers allowed. Showers and toilets provided. **Permits**: *Service Loisirs – Accueil Somme, 21, Rue Ernest-Cavin, 80000 Amiens* – tel, 0322922639 fax, 0322927747.

El Cadastre: section A, Conde-Folie, **night fishing** on *lots* no 299, 719, 725, 1112, 142, 6, 845, 718. Section B, *lot* nos 910, 970, 972, 973 at Condé-Folie. Section E *lot* no705 at La Chaussee – Tirancourt, **night fishing** at *lot* no705. All zones are clearly sign posted.

Étang Les Bas Prés, at Condé-Folie. *Étang de Pavry, lots* no 279, 285, 348, 332, at Boves. *Pont de l'Etoile lots* B no1095, 971, 3, 1005, 4, 1006, 6, at Condé-Folie. **Étang de la Commune d'Aveluy**, *lots* AL 4, at Aveluy. Les Parcs, *lot* no82, *Étang Demilune*, both at Ailly-sur-Somme.

Plan d'eau Malicorne: at Abbeyville, **night fishing** from Pres Colart and from public banks from *Pont d'Epagne* and *Pont de Bethune*. **Étang Roland** (9ha): at *Pont St Mexane*, private lake, by river Oise, it has carp to 25kg, many more over 15kg, common and grass carp. 4 rod limit, boats permitted. The gates are closed at night. **Étang du Vicille Somme**: at Albert, aka *Etang de Veledrome*.

How to catch eels at night – a traditional river Somme technique is called ***Pêche al p'lote***, which involves putting loads of worms onto a wool yarn made into a ball shape. It has no hooks and the eels are simply pulled from the water gripping onto the bait.

The town of Bray has some great fishing

Friendly local angling information:	Association pour Pêche les Pêcheurs de Bray
	Marie de Bray-sur-Somme
	80340 Bray-sur-Somme
	tel, 322760085
	email: vilcot-jean-marie@wanadoo.fr

General local	Tourisme: Place de la Liberte
information:	80340 Bray-sur-Somme
	tel, 0322761138 fax, 0322762511

Junior fishing competition held on 28th June.

22nd May *Coup de Pêche*. From 1.30 to 5.30pm, admission is free for 8-16 year olds, 10 euros for adults, poles only, lots of prizes, 1st prize is 100 euros, 1st in class 10 euros. Sounds like fun.

Domaine public water at Bray: 3.3km stretch of river Somme, principally from the weir at Bray to La the confluence with the canal de Froissy at Neuville les Bray. No fishing in public zones 50m either side of barrages. Domaine privee waters: 300m stretch of river Somme, 100m upstream of moulin de Bray, lots 4 to 8.

Étangs du Couchant (domaine prive)– nice town ponds, not big, lakes, no1 (1ha), 2 (80a), 3 (2ha)+5 (80a). 4 rod limit, 2 rods for zander, pike and *silure*. Spinning allowed on Saturdays, Sundays and public holidays, in January, November and December. *Étang no3* - **night fishing** permitted all year from Friday evening to Tuesday morning, and on public holidays (from evening before to morning after) except on south bank (side of pond 4) indicated by two panels placed here. A *silure* was caught weighing in at 30kg and 1.6m long on *étang no3* by Emmanuel Jankcewicz.

Canal de la Somme: domaine public 2nd cat. 4 rod limit, zone from Ham at Saint Valery. **Permits**: Bar Loto Au Relais *and Articles de Pêche Les Plaisirs de la Pêche*, plus many other bars in town of Bray-sur-Somme.

HAUTE-MARNE (52)

Regional angling advice: Fêdêration de La Marne de Pêche (51)
44, rue Titon,
51000 Chalons Een Champagne
tel, 0326765052, fax, 0326682874
email: federation-peche-
marne.51@wanadoo.fr

Regional water authority: Agence de l'Eau Rhin-Meuse
Route de Lessy-Roziérieulles
B. P. 30019
57161 Moulin-les-Metz Cedex
tél.: 03 87 34 47 00
fax: 03 87 60 49 85

École de Pêche: L'ecôle de pêche de Chalons en
Champagne, tel, 0326705052,
open on Saturdays from 2-5pm for
beginners, carpists and fly, closed in
July and August.

Quote from the Haute-Marne department's *Guide de pêche* " Champagne roads will carry you to the edge of green-river channels. Here you will find relaxation in a calm, serene world that only our land can offer. Fish for mysterious trout and catch carp at night on hemp. Big thrill seekers should seek the mythical *silures*. All is possible, it's true!" And who can argue with that?

The Marne region is not just famous for its vineyards and champagne, but also for the river Marne fish. Exceptional angling sport can be found around Vitry la Francois, Chalons en Champagne, Epernay and Dormans, to name but a few locations. There are 3,474km of rivers and 4,800ha of plan d'eaus and lakes. It has a good reputation for pike fishing. The steep increase in numbers of *silure* is a new feature of the river Marne. **Accomodation**: www.gites-de-france-hautemarne.com

Regulations and Licenses: *Carte Jeunes*, under 16's – 24 euros. *Carte Vacances* – 30 euros, valid from 1st June to 30th September, 4 rod limit on

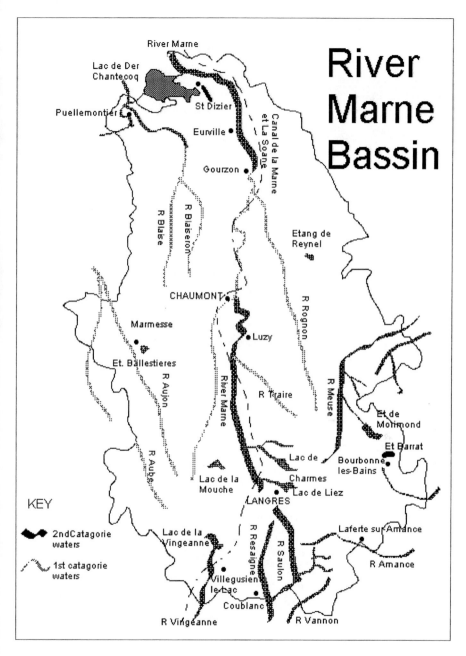

2

2nd cat waters. *Carte Journaliere* –valid for 1st and 2nd cat. plan d'eaus, 2nd cat. rivers – it costs 10 euros.

1st catagorie waters are open from 13th March to 19th September. Pike and zander on 1st catagorie waters, open season from 22/3 – 5/10, and on 2nd cat waters from 8/5 - 25/1. 4 rod allowance, on 2nd cat waters.

Where to fish?

The **River Marne** is classed as 2nd cat public water, (coarse fishing, fish any spot) from the north of the department at Saint Dizier south, downstream to Gourzon. From here south to Chaumont the river Marne is classed as 1st cat public water (i.e. trout fishing). From here to the southern boundary of the department the Marne reverts to 2nd cat public water again. Zander caught on the Marne at Moeslains reach 5 kg. Pike are caught in abundent quantities in deeper reaches e.g. around Rachecourt to over 118cm in length. And: upstream of dams and irrigation channels. Carp to 11kg landed around Gudmont. **Permits**: *Décathlon,, avenue du General Sarrail, Saint-Dizier 52100*– tel, 0325960250.

Parrallel to the course of the river Marne is the nearby **Canal de la Marne a La Saône**; which is classed as 2nd cat public. Access is by bridges over the *écluses*. These swims are good for bagging up on small fry with a pole. Nowdays navigation traffic is reduced to four boats per day and on Sundays no boats are permitted.

Night fishing on Canal de la Marne at Joinville: 250m stretch (*lot* 32) from 200m upstream of *Pont de Cent mètres* to 50m downstream of same point. Weekends and public holidays. At Froncles: 300m stretch beginning at *ecluses* no 35 of Brussieres-les-Froncles, and no 36 of Froncles. Weekends, and public holidays. At Curel: 300m stretch upstream of *l'ecluse de Curel*. From Friday through Sunday, and evening preceeding public holidays. From 27th March to 14th

To the east of the department is a section of the **River Meuse**, classed as 2nd catagorie public water. This can be fished from the north at Harreville les Chanteurs south to Coiffy-le-Haut and again from Bourbonne les-Bains down to past Fresnes-sur-Apance. Pike fishing is particularly good downstream of Bormant. Here the narrow channel and lush aquatic vegetation favours spinning in the shallows. There is between 300 and

600kg of fish per hectare of water. Carp caught at Goncourt went to 13.6kg.

Lac du Der-Chantecoq (4800ha): pi, ca, za, p/b, te, 2nd cat public, third largest reservoir in Europe, after *barragem Alqueva* in Portugal. Open from; 17th April to 31st January. 72km of shoreline. Surrounded by forest parks there are plenty of water sports available. Water level is highest in April and lowest in October. Lake-bottom is half gravel, half-muddy, there are loads of submerged tree stumps (up to 3 metres tall) so you are often required to enter the water to successfully land that fish, to overcome snags. **Directions**: it staddles two departments and is located between Vitry-le-Francois, Saint Dizier and Montier-en-Der.

Home to hundreds of superb carp, (10% of total fish population) commons to 20kg+ and mirror carp to 30kg, one recently went to 27.5kg. A zander was landed here to 10kg, 97cm long. Access to the best swims is by boat but bank swims are also very good. *Silure* record for this lake is 166cm. Best caught pike went to 13.75kg. Perch record for lake is a wopping 2.3kg.

Permits: Mme Marie-Odile Deprez – 12, Place Notre Dame, Montier-en-Der – tel, 0325042589. And at: Magasin Frigane, Fabourg du Moulin Neuf, Chaumont 52000- tel, 0325011716. Boats for hire and day tickets at: *la Plage de Nuisement* in July and August – tel, 0326725106 – fax, 0326730695 email: francois.gringuillard2@libertysurf.fr or: info@au-brochet-du-lac.com – or go to: www.au-brochet-du-lac.com based for rest of year at Saint-Rèmy-en-Bouzemont.

Night fishing: 30 swims, from 27th March to 25th September, 21 of these can be accessed by car, the remainder by boat; night fishing swims cannot be fished by daytime anglers. Zone 1: Larzicourt, zone 2: Nuisement zone, 3: Cornee du Der zone, 4: Nemours, zone 5: Eglise Champaubert, zone 6: Basin Sud, zone from 27th March to 27th November.7: Stade Nautique, zone 8: Est Port Giffaumont. For safety you must not cast more then 100m.

Night fishing permits from: Maison des Pêcheurs
UFAPPMA, Station Nautique
51290 Giffaumont-Champaubert
tel/fax, 0326726343
email: pecheuder@pecheuder.com
or: pecheuder@wanadoo.fr

Why not visit the local *Maison du Poisson*, which has fresh water aquariums and **école de pêche**. Address: *Maison du Poisson, D13 – 51290 Outines*, tel, 0326740000, email: m-o-p.accueil@wanadoo.fr-internet or go to: www.m-o-p.fr.ot they will teach your kids how to catch the big carp in this lake. 4 kiddies fishing competitions: for 7-14 year olds organised on Tuesday of 13th and 27th of July and 10th and 24th August.

For these activities contact Helene or Sylvian – tel, 0326726343. They are based at the separate *Station Nautique* located on the lake, address is given at bottom of page 90, email: lac.du.der.ufappma@libertysurf.fr

Étang de la Horre (331ha): 2nd cat public, located near Puellemontier and Lentilles, carp fishing from 15th March to 15th October, specimens caught over 15kg.   For **more information** contact: *Centre de Pêche en Champagne- 10700 Troujans*, tel, 0325373115, fax, 0325373614.

Langres area; **Le Pays Des 4 Lacs**, have excellent reputation for pike and carp fishing. **Permits**: Expo Pêche – Faubourg de la Colliniere, Langres 52200– tel, 0325870100.

Local information: Tourisme du Pays de Langres
Square Olivier Lahalle B.P. 16
52201 Langres Cedex
tel, 0325876767 – fax, 0325877333
email: tourisme.langres@wanadoo.fr
http://www.tourisme.langres.com

Lac de Charmes (197ha): 2nd cat public, pi, ca, te, pe, situated 8km north of Langres. Open from 27th March to 14th November. Zander were recently introduced here in 2000 and they now reach 70cm and around 4/5kg. Spin for them from a boat from the bridge towards the *baie de Champigny*. *Silure* record for this lake is 133cm. Pike caught to 14kg.

Carp to 22kg. Electric motors only. Boat day ticket is 15 euros. This lake has plenty on offer, including a **campsite** at Hautoreille, 3 restaurants, barbeque areas, and beaches. Plus a hotel de Bourgogne just to the north at Neuilly L'Eveque on the *RD 35*.

Night fishing zone1. For 600m stretch, from 20m downstream of the *digue du CD 74* to 620m downstream of this same point. Zone 2. 400m stretch, 450m downstream of *la digue de la D4*, left bank to 80m upstream of toll bridge (*baie de Champigny*). Zone 3. 100m stretch around water level of the *baie de Varbeton*. Zone 4. 150m stretch, 350m upstream of the reservoir channel to 200m downstream of this same channel. Showers available at **Camping** Hautoreille.

Lac de la Liez (290ha): 2nd cat public, pi, ca, a beautiful lake situated 5km east of Langres. Maximum depth is 14m. Holds regional pike record at 17kg, 3000 pike are caught annualy Several big carp to 20kg+, biggest was 24,5kg. The *Masters Media Carpe 2001* final took place here. Boats for hire at: *Liez Loisirs – Port de la Liez at Peigney* – tel, 0325870903. And at: *Nautic Peigney, 18 Rue du Mont at Peigney* – tel, 0325871394. Buy your day tickets here as well. Electric motors allowed. 15 euros for boat day ticket.

Night fishing: zone1: 400m stretch at Le Ralet, from 27th March to 30th April and from 26t June to 14th November. Zone 2: 500m stretch at Bois Chaupsin from 27th March to 14th November. Zone 3: 600m stretch at Les Sources, from 27th March to 27th June and from 28th August to 14th November.

Lac de la Vingeanne (199ha): aka Lac de Villegusien, 2nd cat public, pi, pe, ca, te, br. **Directions**: 12km south of Langres on the Dijon highway, easy access from the east. Pike caught to 15kg. Carp to 11kg. **Permits**: *Café du Lac, Place Centrale, Villegusien* – tel, 0325884612. Electric motors only. Boat day ticket costs 15 euros. **night fishing**: zone 1: 200m stretch at La Grande Rieppe, zone 2: 200m stretch at Les Etaules. From 27th March to 14th November

Lac de la Mouche (94ha): 2nd cat public, aka Lac de Saint-Ciergues, pi, ca, pe, the smallest of the four lakes, but very nice. Not as many anglers visit here as they do at the more famous other lakes. There is a long walk

from the car park. Pike caught to 15kg. Carp to 14kg. Electric motors only. No boat day ticket required. Facilities on offer: **Camping** P.T.T. toilets, and a barbeque area. **Night fishing**: 1500m stretch divided between locations at Les Roches and Le Bois. From 27th March to 14th November. **Directions**: It is located 6km west of Langres by St-Ciergues, and Perrancey
Private lakes

Les étangs d'Andelot: 1st and 2nd cat private, two lakes, one is trout. Picnic area and kiddies playground. **Permits** from: *M. Pascal, 52700 Andelot* – tel, 0325030786.

L'étang des Lacheres at Montrot: 2nd cat private, at Arc-en-barrois, zander to 15kg. Two lakes (2ha, 1ha) Open all year, 5 euros day ticket, half price for under 16's, under 11's go free, must be accompanied, barbeque area. **Permits** from: *Foyer Rural, 52210 Arc-en-Barrois* – tel, 0325018286, or *Le Relais* – tel, 0325025343.

L'étang de l'Abreuvoir: 2nd cat private, at Chantraines, open from 1st Sunday in May up to last Sunday in october. **Permits**: *Mairie de Chantraines*- tel, 0325319573, or *Chez le Regiseur* – tel, 0325019156.

Étangs de la Ballastiere: 2nd cat private, at Villiers-en-Lieu, 5 lakes (48ha total) carp over 22kg, plus koi carp, *silure* up to 60kg (2m long), koi carp and trout from 24th Febuary to 5th May up to 2.7kg. 22 swims are available for **night fishing** after reservation, 2 anglers per swim. Barbeque area, mini golf, kiddies play area, walking route. **Permits**: tel, 0325563922.

L'étang de Cogirnon: 2nd cat private, at La Belle Fontaine, barbeque area, 3 euros for day ticket, open from March through November. **Permits**: *Mme Martine* – tel, 0325885247.

L'étang du Breuil (4ha): 2nd cat private, at Marac, tr, ca to 13kg, pi, te, pe, dayticket is 7 euros, 10 euros **per night**, free for wives and children under 12.Games area for kiddies free to family of fishermen. Caravan park, 77 euros per week with free fishing. **Permits:** tel, 06815898 or contact: *M. Bernard*, 52260, *Marac* – tel, 0325847651.

L'étang de Chenot: 2nd cat private, at Marac, pi, ca, te, barbeque area, open from 15th June to 15th September, day tickets are 5 euros, under 13's go free but must have adult with them. **Permits**: *M. Clerc* – tel, 0325847507 or *M. Ramaget* – tel, 0325847562.

Les étangs des Ballastieres: 2nd cat private, at Marmesse, pi, ca, za, p/b, 3kg groundbait limit per day, **night fishing**, open 10th January through 20th December, 3 rods, night fishing costs 12 euros for 24 hours. **Permits**: *M. Bernard Vignot* - tel, 03225019433/0325019433..

Les étang de Morimond: 2nd cat private, at Fresnoy-en-Bassigny, pi, za to 6 kg, ca to 18kg, day tickets 8 euros, boat permits 8 euros, barbeque area, bar and restaurant with lakeside terrace, walking tracks. **Permits**: *M. Brauen, Restaurant de Morimond, 52400 Fresnoy-en-Bassigny* – tel, 0325908086 – fax, 0325888528.

L'étang de Reynel: 2nd cat private, pi, pe, big *rotengles*, big *gardons*, ca, open all year, day tickets: 6 euros for one rod, 10 euros for two, **night fishing**. **Permits**: *M. Aubertin Fabrice* – tel, 0329060847 or 0670580435.

L'étang de Savigny (30ha): 1st and 2nd cat private, tr, ca, pi, pe, te, barbeque area to cook your caught trout, 2 rod limit, open from March through November, 5 euros day ticket. **Permits**: *M. Armand* – tel, 0325888051.

L'étang de Terre Natale (1ha): 2nd cat private, at Champigny-sous-Varennes-sur-Amance, pi, ca to 17kg, pe, tr, te, ga, ro, ab, go, night fishing , day ticket 5 euros, 2 rods, **night fishing** 10 euros. **Permits** are available on site.

L'étang de la Juchere (1ha): 1st and 2nd cat private, at Villars-Santenoge, barbeque area, ga, ro, ca, te, go, day ticket 5 euros. **Permits** available on site.

LOIRE ET CHER (41)

The River Loire channel is very wide especially after Orleans. Do not be put off by its size but do bear in mind that big river tactics are *carte de jour*. This means bulking up on your tackle. Some fish can be caught under your nose but other swims require strong casting. The fight of a 10kg river carp 50m out, in strong current is something to remember.

Regulations and Licenses: *Carte Journaliere – plan d'eau* 1st and 2nd catagorie – 7 euros. *Carte Vacances –* 27 euros. *Carte Jeune –* (over 16 less than 18) – 22 euros. *Carte Bleue –* (under 16's) – 1 euro. Pike and zander close season 25/1 – 8/5. 2nd catagorie 4 rod limit.

2nd catagorie public waters: Rivers Loire, Le Cher, Le Canal de La Sauldre, Le Beuvron on left bank downstream of pont de Conde/Beuvron at confluence with La Loire.

Regional angling advice:	Confêdêration du Loir et Cher de Pêche (dept. 41)
	11 rue Robert Nau-Vallee Maillard
	41000 Blois
	tel, 0254902560, fax, 0254902565
	email: fed.peche@wanadoo.fr
Water authority for region:	Agence de l'Eau Loire-Bretagne
	Avenue Buffon - B.P. 6339
	45063 Orleans cedex
	Tél.: 02 38 51 73 73
	Fax: 02 38 51 74 74

Disabled Access

1. Plan d'eau de Lunay, 3 swims.
2. P/d de St Quentin, 2 swims.
3. P/d de Riottes, 4 swims.
4. P/d de Saint Firmin, 3 swims.
5. P/d de Blois Vignault, 2 swims.
6. P/d d'Aze, 1 swim.
7. P/d de Rougeu, 1 swim.
8. Basin du Canal at Noyers/Cher, 3 swims

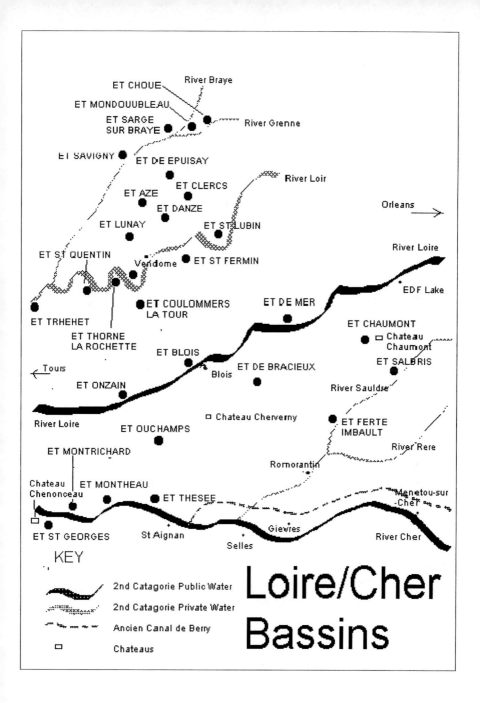

ET CHOUE
River Braye
ET MONDOUUBLEAU
River Grenne
ET SARGE
SUR BRAYE
ET SAVIGNY
ET DE EPUISAY
ET CLERCS
River Loir
ET AZE
ET DANZE
Orleans
ET LUNAY
ET ST LUBIN
ET ST QUENTIN
River Loire
Vendome
ET ST FERMIN
EDF Lake
ET COULOMMERS
LA TOUR
ET DE MER
ET TRHEHET
ET CHAUMONT
ET THORNE
LA ROCHETTE
Chateau
Chaumont
ET BLOIS
ET SALBRIS
Tours
Blois
ET DE BRACIEUX
ET ONZAIN
River Sauldre
River Loire
Chateau Cherverny
ET OUCHAMPS
ET FERTE
IMBAULT
ET MONTRICHARD
River Rere
Romorantin
Chateau
Chenonceau
ET MONTHEAU
ET THESEE
Manetou-sur
-Cher
ET ST GEORGES
St Aignan
Gievres
River Cher
Selles

KEY

2nd Catagorie Public Water

2nd Catagorie Private Water

Ancien Canal de Berry

Chateaus

Loire/Cher Bassins

To your right is the river Loire as you drive west toward Blois from Muides sur Loire. Along the way there is a boat marina that is stuffed to the gills with good size carp. If you get fed up with the idea of the Loire, then try here or, catch *silure* from the cooling reservoir at the EDF nuclear power station by St Laurent Nouan. The local anglers are always keen to show the visitor photos stuck to the inside of their Citreon vans that depict their all-time great *silure* catches, many over 60kg. These fish are considerably better looking than their captors.

Why not kill two birds with one stone, by taking friends and family to visit the delightful Chateau de Chenonceau, east of Bleré it spans the truly beautiful river Cher. It is full of fish that can be clearly seen just by looking over the embankment. The drive back along the river road reveals many fine restaurants for the evening meal and of course some great views over the river Cher. Chateau Cherveny has the best interior to see, it is 20 minutes drive south from the Loire at Blois.

Les Plans d'Eau of the local AAPPMA – 1st cat. – 2 rods, 2nd cat. - 4 rods. All these lakes can be easily located by asking a friendly local to point at your Michelin map. If he can read!

Vallee du Loir: **Aze** (2.5ha), **Choue** (3ha), **Coulommiers La Tour** (0.8ha), **Danze** (1ha), **Danze-La Ville Aux Clercs** (2ha), **Lunay** (4ha) carp to 27kg, **Mondoubleau** (2ha), **Montoire St Quentin** (4ha), **Naveil Riottes** (16ha), **Pezou-Les Fontaines** (6 plans d'eau, 5ha), **Saint Firmin des Pres** (7ha) **night fishing**, **St Ouen** (2ha), **Sarge sur Braye** (0.5ha), **Savigny-Epuisay** (1ha), **Savigny** (0.5ha), **Thorne-La Rochette** (0.5ha), **Trethet** (12ha) **night fishing.**, **Villiers sur Loire** (15ha). Etang St Quentin, **night fishing**.

Vallee de La Loire: **Blois** (5ha), **Bracieux** (0.5ha), **Chaon** (1.5ha), **Chaumont/Tharonne** (1.5ha), **Chemery** (0.5), **Ouchamps** (7ha**), Chouzy** (1ha), **Mer- Les Bordes** (12ha), **Onzain** (0.5ha).

Vallee du Cher: **La Ferte Imbault** (2.7ha), **Monthou-Bourre** (2ha), **Montrichard** (1.8ha**), Montrchard** (10ha), **St Georges** (1ha**), Salbris** (2.5ha), **Thesee** (0.7).

Étang des Berthiers (9ha): at Sauvigny en Sologne, private water, **night fishing,** carp and grass carp, toilet and shower. For **permits**: tel, 0254880758 fax, 0254889246.

Étang Merault (2ha): English owned, good stock of big carp, lake record is 23kg, toilets, showers and cooking facilities on site. No nut baits allowed!

Night fishing on the River Loire at Blois: "there are many sandy banks, the channel is 1.5m to 2.5 m deep and 300m wide! The barrage gates are shut in July and August to form a large shallow expanse of water for the holidaymakers to enjoy watersports. The sailing conditions are very pleasant, it is a good way of spending an afternoon before the night fishing session begins.

Carp fishing is good in this zone, they exceed 20kg, there are also barbel, *silure*s, lots of *l'amour blanc* and *chevesnes*. Common carp are in the majority, catch them with potato. Avoid red boiles unless you want a net full of *chevesnes*. Sweetcorn is better, tiger nuts are a good bait for amour blancs, flesh coloured boiles are recommended but all types work well here. Be careful with your property at night, as you should in every location." – Blois angling club.

Night fishing on the rivers Loir and Cher

River Loire (2 zones)

From a point 50 m upstream of *barrage au Camping de la Chaussée Sainte Victor* up to Fer road bridge (from 1/01 to 31/5).

At Blois left bank from a point 50 m upstream of *barrage de Blois* up to *l'embouchure du Blois* marina (from 1/06 to 31 /12) and on right bank 50m upstream of *barrage*, at campsite by St Victor highway, at a point marked by the railway bridge

River Cher (3 zones)

At Saint Aignan dur Cher right bank upstream of *barrage de St Aignan* for a distance of 400m (seek municipal consent for your bivouacs)
At Noyers sur Cher right bank at place known as *les tuileries* 700m stretch.

At Selles sur Cher left bank at place known as *le Rivage* 380 m stretch.

River Cher, at St-Romain-sur-Cher – right bank, from *l'embouchure du ruisseau* (outflow pipe) du Bray up to *l'écluse de la Méchinière*.

River Cher at Châtres-sur-Cher and at Mennetou-sur-Cher from a place known as *Villecoiffier* at Châtres up to *Pont du Cher* at Mennetou 770 m stretch.

River Cher, left bank at St Georges sur Cher: from a point 440 m upstream of *l'ecluse de St Georges/Cher* down stream to *l'écluse* of the same name.

River Sauldre

At Romorantin right bank at the end of *camping at l'ile des Poulie* to shortly there after. *Le Canal du Berry* At Langon to a place known as *bief duhaut*.

River Loir (2 zones)

At Vendome left bank 10 m upstream of N10 roadbridge for 110m. Saint Hilaire la Gravelle right bank to a place known as *les prés de la chausée* for 130m More lakes: **Saint firmin des Pres** (7 ha) Tréhet (12 ha) **Plan d'eau de la Chesnaie à Salbris** (2.5 ha an eau) - *remise des Carpes* *à* *l'eauasiréne.*

INDRE ET LOIRE (37)

Regional angling information:	Fédération de l'Indre-et-Loire 25 rue Charles Gille – BP 7 0835 37008 Tours Cedex 1 tel, 0247053377, fax, 0247616942 email: federation.de.peche.37@wanadoo.fr

This *département* contains 2,000km of rivers and plan d'eaus accessible. 20 species of fish. Night fishing permitted in designated areas. *Poisson blanc* on all waters. Pike, and zander on *La Vienne, La Loire, Le Cher* and *La Creuse*. Carp and *silure* on the rivers Loire and Le Cher. Trout in

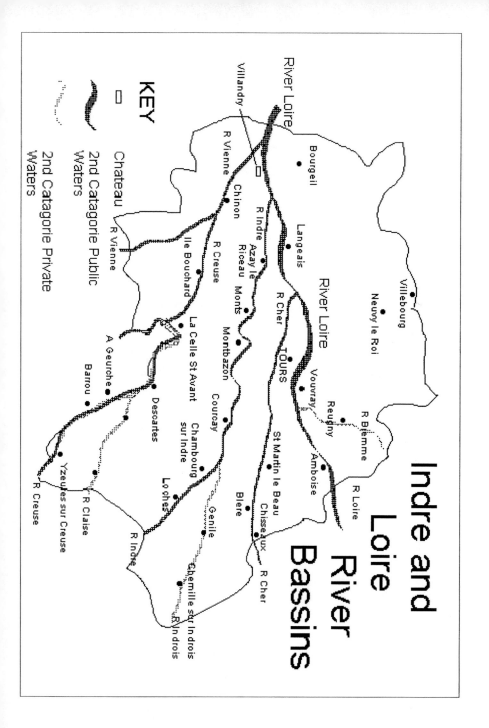

Indre and Loire River Bassins

KEY

▨ Chateau

〰 2nd Catagorie Public Waters

⋯ 2nd Catagorie Private Waters

River Loire

Villandry

R Vienne

Chinon

R Vienne

Ile Bouchard

R Creuse

A Geurche

Barrou

Azay le Riceau

R Indre

Monts

Montbazon

La Celle St Avant

Descartes

Yzeures sur Creuse

R Creuse

R Claise

Coucay

Chambourg sur Indre

Loches

R Indre

Chemille sur Indrois

R Indrois

Bourgeil

Langeais

R Cher

River Loire

TOURS

Vouvray

St Martin le Beau

Genile

Blere

Chisseaux

R Cher

Neuny le Roi

Villebourg

Reugny

R Bienme

Amboise

R Loire

north of dept. on the rivers *Escotias, Le Long, La fare, La Maulne, La Desne* and in south of *dept.* on *l'Aigronne* and *La Creuse*; these are all lovely rivers to fish.

The river Loire holds many good-size carp to 10/11kg and occasional 20kg. However, if you find the experience of fishing the big river Loire a little overwhelming then try the nearby rivers Vienne, Cher and Creuse. They offer great angling sport in truly wonderful settings. My tip is to pick your spot by driving along each channel. There are plenty of locations to choose from.

Chinon is a good base for fishing the river Vienne. There are carp and pike here to 13kg, zander well in excess of the British record, tench and chub to 3kg, roach and even black bass. And hardly anyone fishes here. The nearby Chateau Villandry to the east is the one with the famous gardens, it is right by the river Loire. So be sure to pack your rods.

River Loire basin: **night fishing** on all the following sections All these waters are controlled by local branches of *AAPPMA*. All are 2nd catagorie domaine public unless stated. Species present for all region include *poisson blanc*, carp, bream and pike. Additional species, where indicated.

Amboise: river Loire, 18km public stretch, right bank from (at: Cangey, Limeray, Amboise, Nazelles, Négron and Noizay) to (at: Mosnes, Chargé, Amboise, Lussault sur Loire "*Husseau*"). (17.35 km stretch).

Lakes: Poce sur Cisse (1.5ha) open fron 6/4 – 31/12. **La Moutonniere** (2.5ha) 30/3 – 31/12, day ticket. **Reugny** (1.5ha), day ticket, **night fishing** 27/4 – 31/12. **Villedomer** (3ha) day ticket, 1/4 - 32/12. **Ecôle de pêche** at *MJC d'Amboise, Centre Charles Peguy, rue d'Enterpont, 37400 Amboise* tel, 0247570636. *Club Carpe – Bernard Rodrigues, 9 rue des Tilleuls, 37530 Limeray* tel, 0247301528. **Permits**: *VVF – 1, Rue Rouget de l'Isle – 37400 Amboise –* tel, 0247571979.

Villedomer, Plan d'Eau de l'Arche (12ha): aka Lac de Chambrey les Tours, **night fishing** on all of plan d'eau, reservations required, private water, well stocked 12 years ago, many fish now reach 14-18.5kg. Recently restocked with 1 tonne of carp in 2001, averaging 6-8kg. Best fish at recent enduro went to 15.3kg. **Permits***: Restaurant Roman - La*

Grand'Vallée - 37110 Villedomer – tel, 02.47.55.01.05. **Directions**: 15km north from Tours,

What to see: sightseeing trips to *Chateau d'Amboise, Musee de la Poste, Pagoda, Aquarium de Lussault*. The local *Aappma* also manages angling waters at Limeray on the river Cisse and river Amasse at Amboise.

Vouvray, Rochecorbon, Montlouis sur Loire, la Ville aux Dames, St Pierre des Corps: river Loire, (17.35 km stretch) barbel and *silure*. at St Pierre, right bank. **Permits***: Bar du Musée - Mme Anfray - 26 Rue du Commerce – 37210 Vouvray – tel, 02.47.52.72.24.*
Tours: river Loire, 12km stretch, *silure* and barbel. *Club Carpe de Touraine – Dominique Bellot, 65 Route de Chinon, 37800 Noyant de Touraine*, tel, 0245658247.

Lakes: **Étang du Gardon-** day ticket. **Lakes at Ambillou**: étang communal, etang de Radoire, etang de Givry. **Etang communal**, at Nouzilly. **Étang du Gardon Tourangeau**, at St Branchs. **Etang de la Rainiere**, at Neville Pont Pierre. **Permits**: *Jardinerie Pêche JPC - 17 rue du Général Mocquery - 37550 St Avertin*.

Tours ii: river Loire, 2.4km public stretch, right bank from *Pont Napoléon* to after *Pont de la Motte*. Visit the Tours aquarium.

Tours iii: river Loire, 7.75km stretch, *silure*, barbel.

Langeais: river Loire, 13.4km stretch, a) (1.1km stretch). Left bank – at Villandry – at the fall after *la réserve des Navets* and *l'Ile des Raguins*, aka Les Grandes Levées (from the big lock) up to place known as *les Roberts* at La Chapelle towards Naux Lot ii.2 (300m stretch). And 300m stretch of right bank - *de la cale des Laveuses* (150 m. upstream of *Pont de Langeais*) to the water purification plant (150 m. downstream of *Pont de Langeais)*. Barbel, zander and *silure*.

Lakes: **Lac de Langeais** (3ha), day tickets bought on bank, zander, no night fishing. **Camping** at: Parc de Loisirs (it has a plan d'eau of 3ha). Visit Chateau de Langeais. **Permits**: *L'Univers des Pêcheurs - Magasin d'articles de pêche - 9 Rue Charles VIII- Langeais. Décathlon – 26 rue Georges Melics, 37100 Tours* - tel, 0247490504.

Ingrandes de Touraine: river Loire, 12km stretch, *silure*.

Lakes: **Etang des Gravets** (0.8ha) open from 1st weekend in April to 31/12. **Carte journaliere** – 4.5 euros. **Permits**: *Magasin Vival - Chasse-Pêche - 37140 La Chapelle sur Loire* - tel, 02.47.97.36.39.

Chouze-Bourgueil: river Loire, 14km stretch, lots i6, i7, *silure*. Visit the *Abbaye de Bourgueil*.

River Cher – canalised channel

Blere: river Cher, 7.5km stretch, *silure*, **night fishing**.a). Right bank at Chisseaux: 100 m upstream of barrage de Chisseaux to border of département de l'Indre et Loire, 800m stretch. b) left bank: from *Pont de Civray*, on 700m public stretch downstream. c) left bank - from *Pont de Bléré* to *Riusseau des canaux* (500m stretch). d) left bank: 300 m upstream of *Barrage de Vallet* to Fontenay road (400 m stretch). *Club Carp de la Vallee du Cher – Stephane Gullard*, tel, 0254321833. Visit the *Chateau de Chenonceaux* (one of the best). ***Camping** next to river Cher – tel, 0247579260, it has a pool. **Permits**: *Articles de Pêche - 1 Place Charles Bidault - 37150 Bliere* – tel, 02.47.57.90.41.

Saint Martin le Beau: river Cher, 4km stretch, lots 5&6.

Tours: river Cher, 5km stretch in total, a) left bank at Azay-sur-Cher: from upstream of *Pont d'Azay-Sur-Cher* to *la réserve du Barrage de Nitray* (3,4 km stretch). b) at Larcay, (800m stretch) left bank – upstream of *barrage de Larçay* to 250 m downstream of *barrage de Roujoux*.

Lakes: **les Grand Chenes** at Reugny. 2 lakes covering 6ha, **day tickets** from *restaurant La Cremaillere* at Reugny tel, 0247529404, costs 3 euros (trout fishing – 6 euros), open all year. Zander and tench. **Permits**: *Mondial Pêche - rue Henri Potez – Chambrey Le Tours* – tel, 02.47.48.14.21. **Directions**: route D46 towards Neuille de Lierre,

St Pierre: river Cher, 5km stretch, *silure*, day ticket. **What to do**: visit Chateau de Veretz. Boat trips – tel, 0247503012 (Marie).

Tours: river Cher, *silure*. at Larcy (3 km stretch). Right bank – from road located between Lac Mineur and Lac Majeur des Peupleraies, to the *Réserve du barrage de Larçay*.

River Cher, proper.

Tours: river Cher, 3.5km stretch, *silure*.

Tours i: river Cher, 16.5km stretch, zander. (5 km stretch) right bank at Larcay from *Pont de la déviation* to *Grand Moulin*. Lakes. **La Sabliere**, **La Riche** – open all year, 2 rod limit, under 16's go free, no camping, no night fishing. **Etang de la Membrolle** closed 1/1 – 15/3. **Permits**: *Touraine Pêche 173 Avenue Maginot -37100 Tours* - tel, 0247512651

At Chiseaux, right bank 100m upstream of *barrage de Chisseaux* up to the dept boundary (800 m stretch)

River Vienne

Local angling advice:
AAPPMA de Chinon
Faubourg St Jacques
37500 Chinon
tel, 02479833816.

Trogues: river Vienne, 15.6km stretch, zander. There's a plan d'eau upstream of *barrage du Bec des Deux Eaux* (ski nautic).

L'Ile Bouchard, river Vienne, *sliure*, zander. at L'Ile Bouchard (3 km stretch) Right bank – from *Pont d'Ile Bouchard* up to *Ruisseau le Ruau*. **Permits**: *Graineterie-fleurs-pêche- 5 bis Rue Carnot - 37220 l'Ile Bouchard* – tel, 02.47.97.07.66. **What to do**: the village of Crissay sur Manse is a nice place to visit. Visit the *Chapelle St Couts de Champigny sur Veuede* (Renaissance building).

Chinon: river Vienne, 12km stretch, zander and *silure*. (2,5 km stretch) Right bank – starting at Quai Pasteur, to *garage de St Louans*.

Lot B10, at **Saint Germain-sur-Vienne** right bank 1.5km stretch upstream, to *Pont de Clan*. The bridge is downstream of *l'ile de port Guyot*

At **Dangé Saint Romain sur les deux Rives** between, downstream from *Pont de Dangé Saint Romain* to 50 m upstream of la Frayère des Ormes (6,2 km stretch).

Lakes: **La Cunette** (3ha). **La lac Mousseau at Avoine** (3ha), **disabled access**, day ticket - 8 euros, open Wednesdays, Saturdays and public holidays. **Ecôle de pêche** (fly-fishing) – *Jacques Giffard*, tel, 0247589702. Visit *the Musee anime du Vin* at Tonnellerie. **Permits**: *Relai des Pêcheurs - M. Robert- St Lazare - 37500 Chinon* – tel, 02.47.93.37.62.

Candes St Martin: river Vienne, 7.1 km stretch, , **night fishing**, big pike, and zander. left bank at St Germain sur Vienne – from downstream of l'Ile de Port Guyot to *Pont de Clan*. **Camping** at *Belles Rives*. **What to do**: two fine chateaus to visit and a nice walk to experience along the town promenade.

River Creuse

Tournon Saint Pierre, river Creuse, 7.5 km stretch, barbel. Channel is 40m wide at most, tree lined banks, very nice spot.

Yzeures-sur-Creuse: river Creuse, bathing spot with possibility of parking right up to bank, zander and barbel. From right bank – downstream of *Iles de Gibault* to upstream of swimming zone.

Lakes: **Étang de Rigolet**. Club Carpe – Michael Berthault, 9 rue Pasteur, 37290 Yzeures-sur-Creuse, tel 02477779444634. **Permits**:*Articles de Pêche - 4 Place du 11 Novembre - 37290 Yzeures sur Creuse* – Tel, 02.47.94.61.85.

Barrou: river Creuse, 5.2km stretch, *silure* and barbel. **What to do**: visit Chateau de la Guerche.

Guerche: river Creuse, 8.4km stretch, zander. Visit Chateau de la Guerche XIII.

Descartes: river Creuse, 10km stretch, zander and *silure*.a) left bank: starting from exit to Buxeuil to *la plage de St Rémy* Right bank: upstream of *parc de Paisies* (swimming zone) to la Claise b) Left bank:

of la réserve to opposite *Pont Henri IV* c) Left bank: from la Roche Amenant to its end. No fishing on reseve d), 50 upstream of barrage to 375 metres downstream, facing the new bridge. **Night fishing** allowed. **Permits**: *M. Touzalin - 65 rue du Commerce - 37160 Descartes* – tel, 02.47.59.71.04.

Calle Saint Avant: river Creuse, 6.4km stretch, at confluence with La Vienne, zander and *silure*. Specifically, fish downstream right bank of *plan d'eau* (2 km stretch); and left bank from *mouille* (wet ground) *de Longueville* up to *Pont de la Nationale 10* (1200m stretch) **What to do**: visit Eglise du XVI.

River Indre and Indrois, at **Genillé** both banks (300m stretch). At Monts, right bank to place known as les fleurioux (400m stretch). At Monts right bank to place known as *Patis* opposite the château (300m stretch)

River Brenne**: Chateau Renault** – Left bank – upstream of bridge to the sluice gate (700m stretch).

Lakes of River Loire Basin

Étang de Ile Perchette (3.8 ha) – small private water, no boat fishing, use car park. Best carp went to 15kg+, 100 siver grass carp between 7-10kg stocked in 1994. **Night fishing** permitted for 48hour period – to **reserve a spot** tel, 0247053377 (*AAPPMA La Libellule*) during week up to noon on Friday. No camping, bivouacs allowed. You will require the night fishing tax stamped on your *Carte de Pêche* in leiu of *Carte Vacance* or *Carte Journaliere*. **Directions**: 15km east of Tours on right bank of Loire at Noizay,

La Ferriere - (3ha), carp and trout, 1st cat water, 2 rods permitted, maggots and groundbait allowed. But please leave all alive bait ingredients out of groundbait as this is a trout water. Open 13/3 on Saturdays, Sundays, Wednesdays and public holidays (after 30/4), open every day after 1/5, closes 10/10. Please use the car park. **Permits** from *Marie de la Ferrier* tel, 0247563197. *Les Hermits* – 1st cat same rules as previous water, **permits** from *Magasin Vival, Place de la Marie* tel, 0247563113. **Directions**: 35km north of Tours.

Chemillee-sur-Indrois – **night fishing** permitted from the dyke, 150m upstream (both banks) to 100m after *la levee*. **N/f permits** tel, 0247053377. Boat fishing allowed in zone of *Moulin de Claude*, after the dyke, from 29/5 – 25/1. No jetskis or power boats. No camping.

Lac de Chateau La Valliere aka Lac du val Joyeux –Public water 2nd cat. 2nd cat. water, **night fishing** on right bank (800 m stretch), **permits**: 0247653377. 2 anglers per peg, 7 pegs in all. Boats permitted from 29/5 – 25/1. **Permits** from *Café du Commerce – 37330 Chateau La Valliere* tel, 0247240028. And at *articles de pêche-appats*, *Place du Champ de Loire - 37330 Chateau La Valliere*. **Directions**: 35km north east of Tours in Encaisse valley. Parts of lake visible from route 749, Chateau La Valliere to Bourgueil.

Lac de Rille (240ha): at Rille, 2nd cat public, pi, za, pe, ca, te, little known to outsiders, the lake is made up of two distinct basins and is a true carping paradise. The lake is located at the borders of Indre-Loire and Maine-et-Loire. **Directions**: 40km west of Tours

1st sector is **Retenue de Pincemaille**, it has hotel, restaurant, **camping**, tennis and miniature children's railway. No boat fishing. **Night fishing** is permitted on the north bank. There is a system of buouys seperating the sector for boat fishing from that from the bank. The stars of this lake are the big carp, specimens over 20kg are not that rare. Tight regulations ensure that it stays that way. The tench go to over 2kg. There are 6 swims (2 anglers per peg) for night fishing, contact the *Fed. de Peche* for **reservations** tel, 0247053377 cost is 8 euros for 24 hours, 16euros fpr 48 hours, 2 anglers per peg limit, no ground baiting.

2nd is **Lac des Mousseaux** (5ha), this area is classified as a site of European interest for birdlife. The lake is 5km long in all and situated by villages of Rille and Chateau-la-Valliere. The average depth is 2m, reaching 5m in the middle. Access roads are very good and it is well sign posted. Indicating which zones to fish in and so on. **Night fishing** on both banks except the bird sector. Night fishing **permits** tel, 0247053377, camping banned, bivouacs allowed, boat fishing permitted, electronic trolling motors allowed in boat zone. No ground baiting, no watersports, please use car park.

Les plans d'eau: Domaine public

L'ile Perchette à Noizay (5ha)
Lac de Chemillé sur Indrois (25ha)

Domaine privé

Étang de l'archeveque (12 ha) **night fishing** only at weekends
Étang d'Autrèche (6ha): private water, well stocked with carp to 17kg+, some sturgeon and grass carp. 4 rod limit, well priced, very popular.
Plan d'eau des Rosiers (6 ha): an easy fish. **Le lac des Bretonniéres** at Joué-les-Tours a water of 20ha and: **Le lac de Chambray-les-Tours** a lake of 10ha

VAR (83) – Cote d'Azur

Regional angling advice:	Fédération du Var de Pêche (83) Immeuble Foch, rue des Deportes BP 104 – 83172 Brignoles Cedex Tel, 0494690556 fax, 0494692680 Email: federation@fedepechavar.com
École de Pêche:	Maison Régionale de l'eau Barjols tel, 0494771583 Email: mrepaca@club-internet.fr This centre runs *école de pêche* and has a couple of fresh water aquariums. It is open Monday through Saturday but closed from noon till 2pm.

The local AAPPMA runs a **fly fishing scool** for 10 to 14 year olds in April.on the river Caramy. And a **coarse angling school**, same age group, from 5th to 9th July at Bauduen on the shore of lac de Sainte Croix. For information on both schemes contact the *Fed du peche de Var.*

Regulations and Licenses: *Carte Vacances* – 20 euros, valid from 1/6 – 30/9. *Carte Journaliere* – 8 euros. *Carte Jeune*, under 16,6 – 5 euros

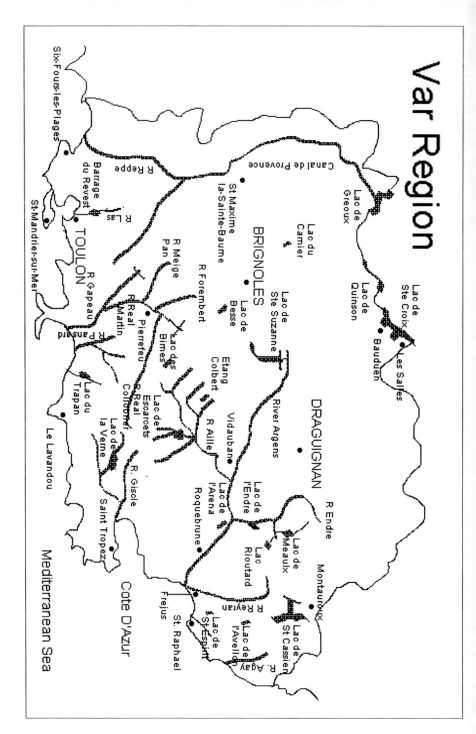

Var Region

1 rod limit for 1st cat waters, 4 rod limit for 2nd cat waters, fishing is banned 50 metres either side of all barrages. 1st cat waters open from second Saturday of March to third Sunday in September, excluding the *Ombre Commun* season; which opens on the third Saturday of May to the third Sunday in Septmember. The use of maggots in 1st cat waters is banned.

2nd cat waters are open all year with exception of pike fishing season; which runs from third Saturday in April to last Sunday in January. You can fish for salmon and trout species in 2nd cat waters but only during the season period stated for 1st cat waters. The use of *comme appâts* or *amorce* is banned on all waters

Carp fishing is permitted on all 2nd cat rivers, lakes and plan d'eaus. Carp are biggest in *Lac de St. Cassien, barrage de Verdon, lacs des Quinson, l'Argens, Sainte Suzanne, Esparron, Revest, and St. Crox.* Smaller stuff in *plan d'eaus of Roquebrune* and *Rouet.* Or try at *lac de Mealx* which has big carp, located after St. Paul en Foret. The *étang de Villepey* by the sea is good for pike, carp and mullet.

Rivers: all 2nd cat public.

River Argens: pi, tr, za, pe, ga, good fishing from Ressars (30m wide channel, 2-4m deep) to the sea. It is good for very large zander, and has a slow current. There is a good head of carp from 10-14kg and some up to 20kg. There are plenty of bream, carp, pike and some black bass. Good spot is at Roquebrune: it is a beautiful location. Here you have the choice of fishing two gravel pits.

The **Lac de Roquebrune** is the biggest and full of zander. However it is best to fish in mornings and evenings to avoid the activities of adjacent club nautique. Best spot is peaceful, deeper end where the power station's water extraction plant is located.

Lac d'Argens is 1km downstream it has black bass, bream and carp. Best stretch according to locals is from Virginie du Ressart, itself downstream of Roquebrune, for 2km stretch downstream to the bridge. In these swims sunken trees hold many big mirrors but you will require strong tackle. *Concours de Pêche* at Fréjus on *l'Argens* on 8th August, tel 0494455626 for details. **Permits**: La Pêche, Rue E. Joly, Fréjus.

River Aille: tributary of l'Argens, tr, pi, za, pe, ga. River Fournel: tributary of l'Argence, pi, za, ga, ca, br, te, bb. River Reyran, la Garonne, l'Agay: za, pi, ga, br, te, bb, ca, mu, al, eel, fish from Fréjus northwards,

River Réal Martin: Pi, te, pe, ee, ga, tr, river stretch from La Portaniere up to the confluence with *le Gapeau – Le Réal Collobrier*, just north of Pierrefeu-du-Var. **Permits**: *Jean Boudou, Magasin de Pêche, hall nautique, Cavalaire.*

River Gapeau: te, ee, ca, pi, ga, per, river stretch from Solliès-Pont downstream to the embouchure with the sea near Hyeres. **Permits**: *Décathlon at, La Garde*, tel, 0494147950.

River Reppe, Las l'Eygouttier: ba, ch, ga, both rivers flow into the Sea, east and west of Toulon. **Permits**: *Le Pêcheur Moderne, Avenue de la Republique, Toulon.*Lakes: all 2nd cat public.

Lac de Besse: l'Issole river basin, pi, ga, bb. **Permits**: *Pêche et Loisirs, M. Martinez, Besse sur Issole.*

Lacs de l'Endre: biggest of two lakes here is 7ha, both hold carp to 15kg, ave 8-12kg. Smaller of two lakes called **Lac d'Aremade**. **Night fishing** permitted all year. **River L'Endre**: Za, pi, pe, te, ca, bb, ga, short stretch from the lake to the confluence with l'Argens. **Permits**: *Tout por la Pêche, Le Muy* tel, 0494451278.

Lac de Sainte-Croix (2200ha) a :massive lake located at Moustieres-Ste. Marie on border with Haute Provence dpt. Key is to locate nomadic shoals of carp off the shoreline. Hotspots at: *Baie de l'ecole de voile* (north end) towards Moustiers, and in *Baie de sales* (south east end). No night fishing but it is still definitely worth a try. **Campsites** by lake. In the early 90's a 25kg carp was reported so this venue has big fish potential. And **lac de Quinson**: **Permits**: *articles de pêche, Verdon*. 5th June, *fête de la pêche* for children at Bauduen. 5th August, *Challenge Germain Garron* for children at Artignosc.

Lac de Sainte Suzanne: aka lac de Carcès, pi, pe, ca, ga, te, **night fishing**. Mainly big common carp up to 18.2 kg, mirror carp to 19kg. **Night fishing** on two zones. 2 campsites by shoreline. *Partie de peche*

aux posson- chat et perche-soleil angling competition takes place on Saturday nearest 28th August, 8.30 am start, for entry contact AAPPMA de Var. Carp enduro in April. **Permits**: *Chasse Pêche Videoo, M. Dalmasso, 32 rue Mal Foch, Carcès* tel, 0494043106. **River Caramy**: short stretch from Lac de Sainte Suzanne to confluence with River Argens, pi, pe, ca, ga.

Lac du Revestidou: le Las basin, north from Toulon, pi, ca, za, pe, te, **night fishing**, Nearby rivers to fish include: **La Reppe, le Las, l'Eygouttier**: ba, ch, ga. **Permits**: *le Pêcheur Moderne, avenue de la République, Toulon*. **Lac de l'Aréna**: pi, za, ca, br, te, bb. 25th July, fishing competition. **Permits**: *Buvette du Lac, M. Perrin, Roquebrune*.

Lac de Saint Cassien: known as *Mecca* for dedicated European carp anglers, Good quality swims, the lake is divided into 3 distinct arms with many inlets. Deepest is northern arm at 44m, western arm is shallowest at 18m, southern arm is 25m deep. There are a lot of large carp present, however it is the most pressurized water in France, even at 450ha! It gets full even in mid winter. Therefore it is recommended that your sessions at this location are planned thoroughly.

It's worth checking out a map of the water from home. This can be downloaded from the internet at no cost so go to http://www.saintcassien.com/ this is an excellent website that is run by Gerard Thevenon who has been fishing here for 20 years. The comprehensive site includes updated records on all the big carp catches, their individual weights, location of catch and what month and year, click on echo banner. You can contact him by email: Gerard@saintcassien.com for free expert advice. Or tel, +33493607034 or if your French is not strong tel, +33497606763 and email: saintcassien@saintcassien.com

Night fishing here is permitted from 2nd Saturday in September to 3rd Sunday in June. Fishing banned in spawning *zone de Fondurane*, upstream of *Rocher de l'Américain* from 1st January to 30th June. Boat fishing permitted all year except in zone de Fondurane from 1st January to 30th June.

Permits: **Camping** *les Floralies, route de la Gare, Montautoux* tel, 0494764403. For night fishing advice: *AAPPMA, M. Thevenon, les Bois*

de Callian – 83440 Tanneron tel, 0493606763/0620020894. **Directions**: autoroute A8 (Nice direction) exit north at *N39* for les Adrets l'Esterel between Frejus and Cannes.

Cassien isn't just for carp anglers. On the 26th and 27th June there is a gala *ChallengeAaux Carnassiers* enties by 11th June, contact *AAPPMA de Var*. 10th July, for *Concours aux silures*: 7th August, *concours aux carnissiers*. Other lakes nearby, **lacs de Méaulx** and **Rioutard**. All waters in this area stock pi, za, bb, ca, ga, br, te, pe.

Lacs des Cous, Sainte Esprit, l'Avellon: located north from Fréjus, pi, za, ga, br, te, bb, ca. 5th September *concours de peche at lac du St Esprit*. **Permits**: *La Pêche, Rue E. Joly, Fréjus. Andat: Au Pescadou, Rue Thiers, St Raphael.*

Lac de Avallan (7.5ha): aka Petit St Cassien, 20 minutes drive away from the big lake, its knickname is due to having a similar shape and terrain. Carp to 10-15kg and a few grass carp.

Plan d'Eau Trapan (70ha): at Bormes-les-Minosas, carp between 14 and 17kg on regular basis, one or two over 25kg. Drained for repairs in 1998. Difficult access. Best swims are a 3-4km walk from car park. However the lake is a short trip from Le Levandou on the Mediterranean coast. No night fishing.

Lac du Broc-Carros (23ha): at Nice, gravel pit close to river Var. Stocked with 900 small carp in 1983 rescued from nearby drought lake. Commons now average 8-9kg, some reach 17kg, with mirrors and leather carp in excess of 22kg. **Night fishing** at weekends and public holidays. Not an easy fish. Boiles only at night. 4 rod limit. **Permits**: *APPMA La Truite Argentee* for information – tel, 1693714761. **Directions**: Lake is situated at end of *ZI de Carros* in *dept* of *Alpes-Maritime just to the east.*

Accomodation: www.gited-de-france-var.fr

American large mouth Black bass were first brought to France from Canada and the United States around 1877. In early days the largemouth was kept to keep carp stocks in check through predation. In 1909 largemouths were successfully imported from Germany to Corance south west of Paris by the Marquise of Ganay. She rightly concluded that this fish species would thrive in the canals of France and therefore proceeded to transfer them to ponds throughout the country.

Years later huge plantings of fry were begun by private owners and fishing clubs all over France. Many river systems received their first plantings from hatcheries built in the 1930's. Silmutaneously bass moved naturally through canals from one basin to another. By 1950 the largemouth was well established in all of the larger river systems.

Presently the largemouth is established in the free waters of the lower Ardour, the lower and middle Garonne, the Charente, the Two Sèvres, the lakes of Landes, most tributaries of the river Loire, the Vilaine, canals in Brittany, the upper Saône to above Lyon, the Rhône near Valence and to a lesser extent in canals connected to the river Seine and waters near the Mediterranean coast.

Largemouth populations are established in most ponds throughout France and in most canals in the extreme north and east. And is relatively successful in central and southern France where there are sizeable sports fisheries in spite of its adversaries found here. However it has failed to become attractive in the eyes of the French angler.

Nonetheless the angler can expect good catches especially in those canals connected to rivers flowing into the Mediterranean Sea because here the favourable climate encourages fish to grow big quickly. A number of excellent sport fisheries exist here as a result.

American smallmouth Black bass were first introduced by Parisian fishbreeders around 1884-1890. At present the smallmouth may possibly persist in the river Meuse near the Belgium border. The Semoise river: a tributary of the river Meuse, has an established population of smallmouths just inside Belgium. Nowdays no stocking or culture of smallmouths is undertaken in France.

PYRÉNEES-ORIENTALES (66)

Regulations and Licenses: *Carte Vacances* costs 30 euros. Under 12's cost 2 euros, 12-16's cost 12 euros. Under 16's *1st catagorie* spinning license costs 22 euros. Pike close season on *2nd catagorie* waters from 25 January till 17th April.

Local angling advice: Fédération de Pêche des Pyrénees-Orientales
Residence Le Belvedère-Batiment Cl
Rue des Callanques
6600 Perpignan
tel, 0468668838
fax, 0468667499
email: federationpeche66@wanadoo.fr

Lac de Villeneuve de la Raho (200ha): at Perpignan. A circular lake not far from the Mediterranean Sea was known for its prolific carp fishing. The water is divided into three by dams. A swimming zone lies to the north. Anglers and boats share a southern zone of 220ha. The third part is a wildlife reserve. Fishing sport is not as good as it was. But you can still strike gold and bag up big time with carp averaging 10-14kg. In recent years fish numbers have gone down but individual size has increased to 20kg on a regular basis. However a 20kg+ carp is a rare event. There are two, **night fishing** zones, a) by the campsite, it is very busy here, b) south shore by Bages; most fish at these zones during the day. Try other areas because the carp patrol close to the bank. 3 rods limit, boats allowed. For more information and night fishing **permits,** contact **Camping** *des Rives du Lac, Chemin de la Serre, 66180, Villenueve-de-la-Raho* - tel, 0468558351. For more information: *Club Carpe 66, Pascal Benoist, 5, Rue Charles – Percier, 66000 Perpignan.*

Barrage d'Agly (170ha): superb for pike, perch and carp fishing. Boats now authorized for whole of lake except around water works zone. **Night fishing** on a 150m stretch from *Pont de Caramy* at Coudala, and on a 750m stretch from the *Ravin del Rach del Cami de St Paul.* Also, on a 100m stretch of left bank downstream of *Pont d'Ansignan* to Ansignan, sign posted. **Directions**: 1 hour west of Perpignan.

Good fishing also at: ***plan d'eaux des Escoumes*** and ***du Soler.***

HERAULT (34) (Montpellier)

Local angling advice: Fédération de Pêche d'Herault
                                Mas de Carles
                                34800 Octon
                                tel, 0467969855
                                fax, 0467880258
                                email: site.internet@pecheherault.com

Rivers: *L'Herault* (d/a tel, 0467969855*) Lergue, l'Orb* and *Vidource.*
Plans d'eaus: a) *le Salegou* b) *La Malhaute* (d/a upstream of Beziers). c)
Lac du Cres, after Castetnau le Lez. d) *Plan d'eau de Pouzols*, river
Herault basin after Gignac. c) *Barrage de Bertrand* on river Herault. d)
Barrage de Meuse on river Herault. e) *Olivettes* on river Peyne f) *Canal
du Midi.*

Regulations and Licenses: *Carte Vacances* costs 33 euros and is
available from 1st June till 30th September. *Carte Enfant* costs 8 euros for
under 16's.

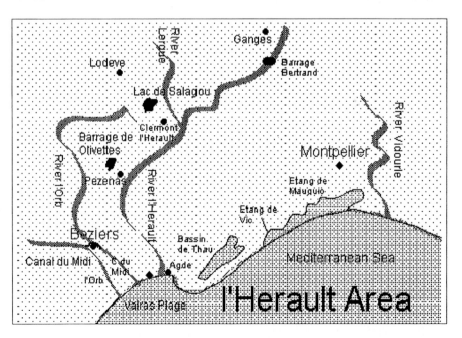

River Herault: mirror carp reach 20kg but there are mostly common carp, 8-14kg sizes are no exception; try fishing from Ganges to the Mediterranean Sea. Carp roam this river, even in the narrow passages through the *Gorges de Herault* where the channel is deep but only 5m wide. Catch carp by the very steep cliffs off narrow shelves. After *Pont du Diable* (a popular swimming hole) the banks become overgrown and difficult to approach. **Directions**: 40km stretch of 2nd *catagorie* river channel between Gignac and Agde. Easier access is by the road bridges at *Retenue de Bertrand*, *Pont du Diable*, the beach at Gignac (D32), at Paulhan (D30), Pezenas (N113), Saint-Lois (D28) and at Agde (D912).

The local *école de pêche* at Agde invites the public to perfect their angling technique. Contact: Luc Séco by email: **guale.agathoise@worldonline.fr**

Plan d'Eau des Olivettes, zander and carp fishing began after their population was established with draining of the reservoir in 2000. The undergrowth was cleared and footpaths built along the shore. **Directions**: Situated at rear of *Pays de Pézenes* the *Barrage des Olivettes* is located on the river Peyne in a valley by the village of Vailhan.

River l'Orb, after the passage through the *Gorges de Roquebrune* the river l'Orb crosses the Bitteroise Plain and becomes 2nd *catagorie* waterway much appreciated by zander and pike fishermen, downstream to the Mediterranean Sea at Vatras Plage. The proximity of the *Canal du Midi* allows pleasure angling for all the family during the holidays.

Parcours Fédéraux at: **plan d'eau Les Sablières de Pouzols** combines 2km of river Herault and 20ha of adjacent *plan d'eaux*. Pike, zander, carp, *poisson blanc,* trout, black bass. **Disabled access**. **Directions**: a few km from Gignac. On border of river l'Herault, 30km from Montpellier, 50km from Béziers, access is from *départementale D32* (road); between Gignac and Bélarga, entrance is opposite village of Pouzols.

Located here is *Le Centre Aquapêche de Pouzols;* which caters for everyone. Visit the educational center that explains the surrounding fauna, forna and aquatic environments. Its *école de pêche* angling school teaches kids how to fish on Wednesdays. Contact: Francois Nicol tel, 0467 965919.

Parcours Fédéraux at **plan d'eau de la Maulhaute**: situated on the river l'Orb upstream of Béziers at Lignan-sur-Orb. This ancient gravel pit was cleaned up in the 1980's and is now good for pike, zander and carp. Easy access to: 1km of river l'Orb and 20ha of *plan d'eaux*.. Two swims have **disabled access. Directions**: several km north of Béziers. To 10km of *l'autoroute A9* (leaving Beziers east), the water is accessed by *départementale D19* between Lignan-sur-Orb and Murviel-les-Beziers.

Lac de Salagou (750ha): 2nd cat public reservoir built in 1968, used as flood control for Herault river system. Setting is sensational and makes this a superb angling destination. Some describe their experience here as mythical, whatever that means. The reservoir is surrounded by red hills, the blue-green water itself turns carmine red after heavy rain. According to local fishermen it contains massive carp specimens (30kg lake record, 10kg ave) there are indeed a lot of carp here. But take note that they have an elusive reputation. They have grown wise to boilies. 70% are hard fighting common carp, the remainder are very big mirrors.

There are dirt roads along most banks - or at least a little back, uphill - but these tracks are certainly not all too easy to navigate by car. This can mean a long walk with the gear to most swims - so reduce it to the minimum! **Remember to carry lots of water in the summer heat**. This of course puts on extra pressure on the relatively few easily accessible swims at the lake - some of which you can actually drive your car directly into and park right next to the water.

Another possibility is of course to embarque all the gear from one of these areas, and simply sail to the more inaccessible spots. Surely only a few anglers do this - and they get the benefit of being able to reach areas with virtually no angling pressure.

Most mornings start with absolutely no wind at all - warm and nice during all the warmer months - and carp can normally be seen and heard jumping an rolling at short regular intervals. With almost no exceptions a while after the surface activity has calmed down a bit, the wind starts to pick up at about 10 or 11 o'clock.

First, a few long and gentle, sweeping blows - and within minutes almost a storm, blowing weed up the lines. In a way this wind is very welcome - as the heat at this time often begins to be quite hard, and some cooling is certainly welcome - but if you're out in a small rubber dinghy watchout! As Gabriel Garcia Marques warns "beware of the *tramontana*."

28km long, average depth is 20m, 22m by the island, 4m deep at *baie d'Octon*, to 45m deep at the dam. Environment benefits from clement Mediterranean climate so fishing at autumn time remains very good, even in deep winter the water temperature stays above 7 c. (28c in summer). Therefore the fish remain active all year and so grow larger than in the rest of France. Many carp caught at 15m to 20 metres depth..

This penultimate point explains why there are a great many pike from 15-20kg (21kg lake record). The majority, are caught on coloured spoons in large inlets, over the submerged village of Celles. A popular spot in winter is at *Parachines* where the lake is at its deepest. The best place for zander and perch is at *Celles zone* around dead submerged trees, catch them with spinners or deadbait. It's also a good idea to cast from a boat towards the shore by steep banks and cliffs. The lake is also good for bream and tench on the northern shore at *Clermont Herault* and *Lia*. The lake record for zander is 14kg. An eyewitness, reports seeing hundreds of carp feeding here in less than 1m of clear water, by bullrushes.

Octon: at the beginning of the fishing season: in April, March and in autumn. The low water level and the excessive weed encourages the carp to leave this bay to go head for cooler water. This exposed sector on the right bank is interesting during stormy weather. The *roselières* (rockroses) shelter migratory birds: *Rousserolle turdoïde*, and large warbler which arrive from Gabon; crested Grèbe with the russet-red plumage as of spring and *grisâtre* in summer... there is a lot going on.

Celles: submerged tree stumps provide perches for the large Cormorants. In the middle is an island, *le château* spot carp on its left bank. The right bank is full of old scrap-metal and its steeper banks provide good winter swims, but are accessible only by boat. The right-hand bank behind the village of Celles is over a shallow shelf. Further on the same side the inlets are also accessible in the boat from the village. On the hillside there are the ruins of an old farmhouse, fish these sectors in summer.

Vailhés: The carp swims are numerous and very good in spring along the shoreline below the village of Vailhés. These gentle banks are windward this is below the *chapelle des clans* after the village of Vailhés.

Pradines: difficult to reach in the car, forest track corroded by the storms, but the effort is often rewarded. You will find very good swims here. This is the last way to reach the bank before the dam. Best swims are found   in the field in front of the large stone heap. In front of these two swims there are long aquatic rushes. Fish in front of them and not behind, indeed it is difficult for carp to cross this dense vegetation.

Liausson: in front of the boat centre some good carp swims. Behind centre in the arm which, goes to the dam there are good swims on the right hand side, but this way is difficult and accessible only in the boat. Below the village of Liausson the shallow banks offer many carp swims. Spring to autumn and especially summer, tents and campers often occupy these banks. The windward shoreline here is good for fishing.

In front, and in the small bay (on the left-hand side) you have beautiful carp swim. These shallow swims are best avoided in summer. By the tower of the Rouens peninsula is very good all year. The profile of the banks is rather broken with steps and accessible only in the boat. The banks of Sure (*montage de auche*) accessible in the boat to fish towards the large feature.

Amorcage: Fish near range: a hundred boilies is better placed than 1 kg scattered. The corn, the hemp seed, the broad bean, in short all the seeds still gives very good results and even potato. There are carps here, which never saw boilies. Don't cook the seeds because they attract bream and gardons, (just a soaking of 48 hours in, hot water to prevent inflation in the stomach of fish). The boilies containing animal flour style fish mix (50% mix neutral + 50% flour fish) quite heavy (even without flesh-colored savour, additives and gravitational) throughout year, the mix is neutral + fruit. The boilies must be hard, of size higher or equal to 20 mm, especially in summer with crayfish about. The use of boilies with a pop up rig is recommended.

A light starting of approximately 100 boilies is recommended. 4 rods out after 12 midnight is enough and if you do not strike during first 24 hours it will be necessary to move your rods a few meters. That is enough, this is not the time to sulk and change swim or go overboard with the loose feed. Sometimes it is enough to retrieve your line and cast to the right or the left, to cause strikes. In fact the carp do not live for boiles, fortunately! With the best boilies with all the possible attractants and additives they still remember their natural foods. First ask why the carp pass by here and not elsewhere to come to feed?

Be careful. Don't bother fishing at distance. Most carp here are hooked within 50 and 100m of the shore. Salagou is packed with rocks and stones - and often they're overgrown with razor-sharp zebra mussels. If you feel the carp pulling the line over these obstacles or any snag out there, don't try to hold it back. This is certain to cut the line. Instead, play the fish gently, let it run and get into free water and lift the line up by itself.

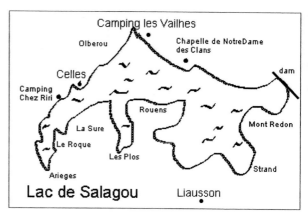

Night fishing: bank only 1/1 – 2nd Sunday in April and 1/6 – 31/12 boat and bank. 4 rod limit. Pocession of nite lite is mandatory. **Permits**: *tabac-presse* opposite the river Lergue in Lodeve, *Carpe Salagou* in Octon tel, 0467960878. Electric boat motors only. Campsites at Chez Riri on west shore near Celles and Les Vailhes on north west shore. Outside July and August it's possible to fish directly from *Chez Riri Camping* where submerged trees offer holding areas for big carp. *Euro Pêche Chasse Paci* located just outside the town centre by the shopping complex at *Le Clos de Madeline* (off *Avenue du President Wilson*) 34800 *Clermont-L'Herault. Tourisme: Clermont l'Herault* tel, 0467962386. **Directions**: After a long journey along la Languedocienne to Montpellier, turn off at Montpellier Sud, towards Millau. This 4-tracked highway takes you to Gignac and further on to either Clermont l'Hérault or Lodéve.

The European record for an albino *silure* was broken on 7th July 2004. Reaching 2.30m in length it took 47 minutes for MonsieurJean-Francois Kronenberg, a.k.a. JFK to land the 81kg ancient and short sighted, female catfish on the banks of the Petit Rhône upstream of Arles. Your local guide: Jean-Claude Tanzilli – tel/fax, 04 78 27 24 33.

FRENCH NATIONAL ANGLING RECORDS

Mirror carp – 37kg caught by Macel Rouviere in 1981 (dpt. 77, Seine-Marne).. Common carp – 33.975kg - the Bulldozer - Michael Brechtmann – Foret d'Orient 1995 (dpt. 77). Koi carp – 12.8kg – Rory Michellend – 2002 – river Saone. *Amour Blanc* – 31.6kg – Guy de Restrepo 1996 (dpt. 67 – Basin-Rhin). *Amour Marhe* – 29.125kg – Pascal Rhein – 1995 (dpt. 67). *Amour Argente* – 36.6kg – Marcel Maubuisson – River Mayenne – 2000 – (dpt. 49 – Maine-et-Loire).

ADDITIONAL INFORMATION

Guide's tip for family holiday angling – Purchase your cheap fishing pole (less than 7 euros) at any branch of Décathlon Sports chain located throughout France. Obtain your sweetcorn bait from the local *supermarché*. Children under 12 usually qualify for a free *Carte de pêche*, those up to 16 years pay half.

Abreviations: pike- pi, carp –ca, zander – za, eels – ee, poisson blanc – p/b, *silure* – si, barbel –ba, tench –te, alose – al, mullet – mu, chevesne – ch, gardons – ga, gouchon – go, rotengle – ro, ablette – ab

Night fishing is permitted in designated areas but not *camping sauvage* (unofficial camping) anywhere. On many occasions an angler's bivvie has been mistaken for illegal camping by an official. However much can be accomplished if you speak a little French.

ACCOMMODATION

Hotels:
http://www.venere.co
http://www.welcomecottaged.com
http://www.francehotelreservation.com
http://www.visitfrance.co.uk

Gites
http://www.gites-de-france.fr/
http://www.visitfrance.co.uk

Campsites/self catering
http://www.geotour.com
http://www.les-campings.com
http://www.supersites.uk.com
http://www.france-camping.eu.com

Car rental: http:/car-rental-france.pedez.co.uk

OTHER TITLES IN EUROPEAN ANGLING SERIES

My first volume curently available is called *Pescando En España* **Angling in Spain**. Reviewed by the Angling Times in October 2003, they said…

"This is the only angling book I've seen on Spain and it contains excellent information on 130 popular angling locations, including the Costa Brava, Costa Dorada, River Ebro, Costa Blanca, Costa del Sol, Costa de la Luz and Canary Islands. This 123 page book deals with top fishery locations, obtaining licenses, and also offers best fishing methods for different waters and advice on where to stay

My second book title also available is called *Pesca a Vara* **Angling in Portugal and More Spain.** The Angler's Mail said in their **** star review 2004…

"The book highlights favourite places to fish for Iberian barbel on the River Guadiana, trout on the Alge River to bass fishing located all over southern Portugal. There's also a sea fishing section, how to obtain a course license and a local sea bass recipe thrown in for good measure". For the new Spanish section I include the regions of Seville, Cordoba, Jaen and Extremadura (Badajoz and Caceres).

The purchase price for each title is £10 plus £1 p+p. Why not buy both titles for £17 including p+p. To find out more or order a copy, telephone Phil Pembroke. 01708 764696. International dialling code - 0033. Or, email myself at: philippembroke007@hotmail.com

CONCLUSION

Experience fishing in beautiful countryside, historic towns and cities, and don't hestate to try all the fine wines and restaurants as you go along. Remember that the aim of an angling holiday in France is France itself. Catching that elusive carp or catfish is an occasion for celebration but still only a secondary goal to experiencing the other great things that are on offer to the visitor. - Tight lines and *bon pêche*, Phil Pembroke